MW01201473

MySQL & JSON

A Practical Programming Guide

Second Edition

Dave Stokes
MySQL Community Manager
Oracle Corporation

ISBN 9781260135442 for first edition

ISBN 978-0-578-78324-6 for the second edition

Chapter 1

Introduction

Once upon a time there was one computer. But since the creation of the second computer there has been a problem moving and sharing data between systems. It took decades of hard work, arguments, negotiations, proposed standards, and a great deal of frustration to get to the point where data transfer between systems is almost trivial. For many years many very smart people argued over ASCII or EBCDIC character encoding, endianness of computer memory, and various standards like SGML and XML. JavaScript Object Notation or JSON has become the favorite way for many of encoding data for moving between various systems. JSON encoded data has several advantages over previous efforts that it is very human readable, easy to parse with programs, and not overly complicated. Other formats such as XML are not as easy to quickly scan with the human eye.

XML or eXtensible Markup Language was widely used before JSON but is harder to scan with the human eye, as can be seen in the example below. It is relatively easy to parse programmatically, it does facilitate data interchange, and it is a vendor independent standard.

```
<message>
    <to>VP Sales</to>
    <from>VP Marketing</from>
    <heading>Remember</heading>
    <body>Don't forget we have a tee time at 8:30 on
Saturday!!</body>
</message>
```

Example 1-1 -- XML example used for the transport of a message.

The coding for XML takes more effort. The starting tag <...> and end tag </...> must match, for example <to>VP Sales</to> and encapsulated properly. Having the entire message between the <message> start and </message> end block can be tedious when written and frustrating when mistyped. JSON's lack of strictness and verbosity by contrast are probably the two most popular reasons in its replacement of XML in the marketplace.

Considering the vast increase in the volume of data being shared every year, it is imperative that the information be shared in an easy to digest format. Having that format easy to produce provides benefits like ease of programming, ease of proof reading or debugging, and low cost of entry. JSON fulfills these roles beautifully.

MySQL has had over twenty years of life before it received a native JSON data type. So like an INTEGER, a DECIMAL, or a DATE there is a way to store an entire JSON document in a column of a row of a schema. MySQL 5.7 arrived with the ability to store roughly a gigabyte of data in a column in a row in a table. Before the native JSON data type there were special schemas or user defined functions with limited JSON support. This new data type has proven to be very popular and has probably been the cause of many sites upgrading from much earlier versions of MySQL to get access to it.

JSON

JavaScript Object Notation or JSON is text based, language independent data interchange format for the serialization of data and is derived from the object literals of JavaScript as defined in the third edition of the ECMAScript Programming

Language Standard. There are actually two standard for JSON: Internet Engineering Task Force's (IETF) Request For Comment (RFC) 7159 (https://tools.ietf.org/html/rfc7159) and the European Computer Manufacturers Association (ECMA) Standard 404 (https://www.ecma-international.org/publications/standards/Ecma-404.htm). The IETF's document is roughly sixteen pages long while ECMA's is five. This is a relatively short set of standards compared to the IETF RFC 5321 for the Simple Mail Transfer Protocol (SMTP) at ninety five pages. But the two standards for JSON are fairly explicit.

JSON has a grammar and it is simple. JSON is a series of tokens – six structural characters ('[',']','{','}',':', and ','), strings, numbers, and three literal names (false, null, or true). Objects begin with a '{' and end with a '}' while arrays start with a '[' and end with a ']'. Colons ':' are used to separate names and values. Multiple objects or arrays are separated by a comma ','. Like Lego blocks, simple components can be combined to make much more complex structures.

The above paragraph describes the attributes but it is easier to think of JSON data being structured as objects with name/value pairs or as an ordered list of values, also known as an array. Most programming languages and their programmers use objects and/or arrays on a regular basis. The simple design of JSON allows it to be independent of the computer language used to generate or read the data.

So what does JSON look like?

JSON documents can be very simple, made up of keys and values.

```
{
   "name" : "Bond",
   "first": "James",
    "ID"  : "007"
}
```

Example 1-2 -- Example of JSON Document

The data is enclosed within braces (**{** & **}**) which tells us
it is a JSON object, not an array which would have the data
within brackets (**[** & **]**). Inside this object are three key/value
pairs -- name/Bond, first/James, and ID/007. All of the data
could have been on one line and still be a valid JSON document
but is formatted as multiple lines for ease of reading. For now
consider all the keys and their values as strings.

UTF8MB4

The JSON specifications mandate the use of the UTF8MB4
character set. This character set allows the encoding of many
languages, graphics, and emoji. Note that UTF8MB4 is an upto 4-
byte character set which means this data can take up four times
as much space as data in a simpler character set such as Latin-
1. In some cases this inefficiency may preclude the use of the
JSON data type despite its rich ability to store a wide variety
of data.

There are four planes (think bytes) that make up UTF8MB$.
The first plane, plane 0, is made up of generic characters and
is known as the Basic Multilingual Plane or BMP. Plane 1 is
the Supplementary Multilingual Plane is SMP and contains

historical scripts such as Egyptian hieroglyphics. Plane 2 is the Supplementary Ideographic Plane SIP, is used for Chinese, Japanese, and Korean ideographs. And the last plane Plane 3 is the Tertiary Ideographic Plane or TIP and contains the CJK Unified Ideographs Extension G.

But all you have to worry about is that all JSON data must be UTF8MB4 and can ignore these details for now.

MySQL

This is not a book on administrating, programming, or using MySQL. You will need access to a MySQL server running version 8.0.20 or later, on a local system or system available over a network. The Community Edition of the MySQL server is FREE under the Gnu Public License, version 2 or GPLv2. The Community Edition is available for Microsoft Windows, Linux, Mac OS, or available as source code. There is a non-FREE Enterprise Edition for customers with support contracts with additional valuable tools for management functions such as at rest encryption, monitoring, and backups. The examples in this book will work with this edition also.

Some of the examples in this book will work with MySQL 5.7 which was the first version of the software with a native JSON data type. However many of the newer features are only found in the later version and MySQL 8.0 is a much superior platform for JSON data.

If you want to install MySQL please follow the directions at https://dev.mysql.com/doc/ and carefully follow the instructions for your operating system platform. You can also install MySQL within a virtualized server or container for the purposes of this book. Remember that you need at least MySQL 8.0.20 to have access to the MySQL functions and older versions may lack some features or have them implemented differently than shown in this book.

And be aware that Oracle Engineers who create and maintain the MySQL server software have evolved the way JSON and the JSON functions work as the standards have changed, users have given feedback on the product, and as part of general improvements in the product. Hopefully all these changes are noted in the text but be aware that the version of MySQL you are running may behave slightly differently than previous or later versions.

Examples on GITHUB

A complete list of examples are available on Gitgub at https://github.com/davidmstokes/MySQLandJSON for you to download. The examples in this book are short and easy to copy from the book into your command line program. However you can copy them from the example listing if that is not an option you wish to pursue.

The CLIs & Examples

This book uses various MySQL client programs or Command Line Interpreters. The *mysql* cli examples usually will include the prompt **mysql>** and the new MySQL Shell or *mysqlsh* will be abbreviated to a prompt showing the mode - **JS>** for JavaScript, **PY>** for Python, and **SQL>** for Structured Query Language.

Oftentimes the examples are shown being entered without command line continuation characters for clarity. Refer to the Github listing of examples if there are questions on the various examples. All the examples shown will work in either *mysql*, *mysqlsh*, MySQL Workbench, or other similar programs so the choice of which to use is yours. The author does prefer mysqlsh and MySQL Workbench.

Data

The examples will mainly use the world_x example data set or can easily be created from the examples herein. The predecessor world database has been used for many years by MySQL in documentation, training, examples, and blogs. After installing the latest and greatest MySQL, please install this data after downloading it from https://dev.mysql.com/doc/index-other.html.

The installation can be done several ways; the most popular two are from an operating system command line and from within the MySQL shell. There are methods but these two are very reliable and simple.

```
shell> mysqlsh -u root --sql --recreate-schema world_x <
/tmp/world_x-db/w
orld_x.sql
```

Example 1-3 -- Installing the world_x database from

the Linux shell

The MySQL CLI program can also be used interactively as can the new MySQL shell.

```
File Edit View Search Terminal Help
dstokes@dstokes-Latitude-E7240:~$ mysql -u root -p
Enter password:
Welcome to the MySQL monitor.  Commands end with ; or \g.
Your MySQL connection id is 10
Server version: 8.0.21 MySQL Community Server - GPL

Copyright (c) 2000, 2020, Oracle and/or its affiliates. All rights reserved.

Oracle is a registered trademark of Oracle Corporation and/or its
affiliates. Other names may be trademarks of their respective
owners.

Type 'help;' or '\h' for help. Type '\c' to clear the current input statement.

mysql> source ~/Downloads/world_x-db/world_x.sql
```

As can be the new MySQL Shell or mysqlsh.

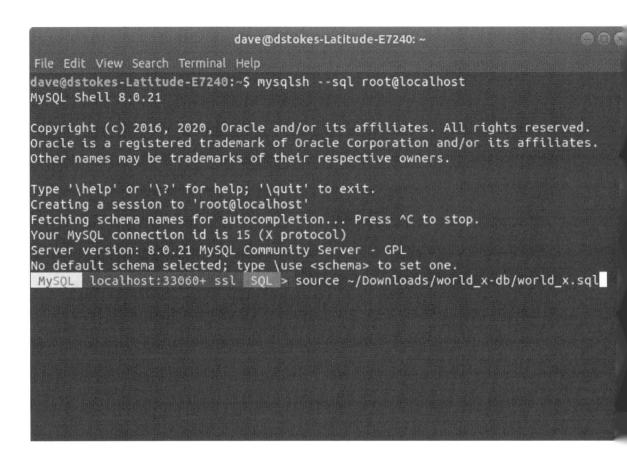

Example 1-4 -- Installing the world_x database from the MySQL Command Line Interpreter and from the MySQL shell

The two shells, the MySQL CLI and the new Shell, work pretty much the same if the mysqlsh program is in SQL mode (use \sql to switch from JavaScript or Python modes into SQL mode).

How to Use This Book

This book was designed for readers to enter the examples on their own installations of MySQL. Some people can learn very efficiently by just reading but many more gain additional insight by typing the examples into their own MySQL instance. The simple examples that follow can easily be deleted later when no longer needed.

The MySQL manual is the definitive reference book on the various features of MySQL. However often the examples are hard to grasp for novices at the start of the learning curve or for the experienced but not in a certain facet. So use this book to backfill areas where the manual is nebulous, confusing, or just not at your level.

Some points like array numbering starting at zero and document pathing are restated over and over again and will be seen as tiresome and pedantic for those reading from the first page through to the last. But many will use this book by only referring to the part of a section that concerns them at the moment. Those folks may be oblivious to warnings on an earlier page or may be dogmatic on these points will save those people grief.

One of the problems in learning computer technologies is learning to understand mistakes. This includes learning to understand error messages and warnings. If you make a mistake in entering one of the examples, examine any messages for clues and then compare what has been entered with what is in this text. It is quite common to miss a single or double quote and transpose keywords when entering Structured Query Language but the server will not simply tell you that you fat fingered. So one must learn to comprehend the error messages to find out where one has goofed. *Do not be afraid to make mistakes!* Mistakes are part of learning and learning to fix mistakes is part of the process. Many martial arts stress that the difference between a novice and a master is that a master knows when a mistake is starting and can rectify it before it becomes a problem. And rectifying fat-fingered commands is a regular occurrence and is a great way to learn to understand what error messages are trying to tell you.

And it is very hard for a static item like a book to keep current with ever changing software. Some of the functions discussed herein have evolved over time and some are in an experimental stage. Please use this book as an addendum to the official MySQL software documentation. The author has tried to make this book as useful as possible but as time marches on the details inside may not reflect the actual software -- and that is actually a good thing.

Any errors or omissions are my one and I take full responsibility for them.

Chapter 2

JSON as String Data, JSON as a Data Type

Long before MySQL 5.7, developers were storing JSON in MySQL and it is still possible without using the JSON data type. They were storing this data in text fields (CHAR, VARCHAR, TEXT, or BLOBs). And this remains a viable option for those running versions of MySQL before version 5.7.

```
mysql> CREATE TABLE foo (oldJson char(250));
Query OK, 0 rows affected (0.32 sec)


mysql> INSERT INTO foo
```

```
        VALUES ('{ "name" : "Bond",
    "first" : "James",
     "ID" : "007" }');
Query OK, 1 row affected (0.04 sec)


mysql> SELECT * FROM foo;
+------------------------------------------------------+
| oldJson                                              |
+------------------------------------------------------+
| { "name" : "Bond", "first" : "James", "ID" : "007" } |
+------------------------------------------------------+
1 row in set (0.00 sec)


mysql>
```

Example 2-1 -- A JSON document stored as a string

This method did allow storage of JSON data. Basically MySQL is storing a string and there is nothing done to validate that this is a valid JSON document, there is nothing to enforce rigor on the data to ensure the correct type of data or value range is being inserted, or is there and way to ensure the tags are consistent, and it can be painful to search. For instance a field for email may be labeled 'email', 'eMail', 'electronic-mail', or one of other dozens of variations. The ability to examine this textual JSON information lies with various string functions in MySQL or programming languages that are often cumbersome.

One benefit of keeping JSON data in a string is that the data will come out as it was put in also known as idempotency. Later in this chapter it will be shown that the native MySQL

JSON datatype 'optimizes' the data and sorts the keys in the key/value pairs so the native JSON datatype does not ensure impotency. If exact regurgitation of the data is need then the JSON datatype should not be used.

Searching can be done using Regular Expressions also known as REGEX. Regular Expressions are often messy, hard to document, and harder to understand. Many developers avoid them at all cost but that is a bit extreme. It is not uncommon to fail to comprehend your own REGEX code written weeks or months before.

```
MySQL  localhost:33060+ ssl  json  SQL > SELECT * FROM foo WHERE oldJson REGEXP 'Bond';
+------------------------------------------------+
| oldJson                                        |
+------------------------------------------------+
| { "name" : "Bond", "first" : "James", "ID" : "007" } |
+------------------------------------------------+
1 row in set (0.0009 sec)
MySQL  localhost:33060+ ssl  json  SQL > 
```

```
mysql>   SELECT *
         FROM foo
         WHERE oldJson REGEXP 'Bond';
+--------------------------------------------------------+
| oldJson                                                |
+--------------------------------------------------------+
| { "name" : "Bond", "first" : "James", "ID" : "007" } |
+--------------------------------------------------------+
1 row in set (0.00 sec)

mysql>
```

Example 2-2 Using a REGEX in a SELECT query. Note the lack of an '=' in the REGEX option.

Regular Expressions can be complicated, hard to read, and harder to comprehend. Many developers are very good at writing Regular Expressions but many more are not. Often they are easy to over complicate and painful to debug. Take the case where the first name of the person sought for is not exactly remembered so the search is written to lock for a 'Jim', 'Jon', 'Jimmy' or 'James' .

```
MySQL  localhost:33060+ ssl  json  SQL > SELECT *
                                   -> FROM foo
                                   -> WHERE oldJson REGEXP 'J*m
+----------------------------------------------------+
| oldJson                                            |
+----------------------------------------------------+
| { "name" : "Bond", "first" : "James", "ID" : "007" } |
+----------------------------------------------------+
1 row in set (0.0006 sec)
MySQL  localhost:33060+ ssl  json  SQL >
```

```
mysql> SELECT *
       FROM foo
       WHERE oldJson REGEXP 'J*m';

+----------------------------------------------------+
| oldJson                                            |
+----------------------------------------------------+
| { "name" : "Bond", "first" : "James", "ID" : "007" } |
+----------------------------------------------------+
1 row in set (0.00 sec)
```

Example 2-3 Using a REGEX with a wildcard character. For an experiment change 'J*M' to 'Fred' to observer the massage for no matches.

This example works in that a record is found. But if the person searching could not remember if the name is 'Jim', 'James', 'Robert', or 'Lynn' this type of search would not help. The regular expression can be rewritten to do so but it gets much harder to interpret. And harder to maintain.

Indexing columns to speed searches is common, popular, and highly encouraged under the right circumstances. Indexing an entire text column (but not blobs) can be done in most circumstances but once again REGEX returns for searching. Very wide index fields take a lot of power to search and the performance is usually much less than what was desired. So do not try indexes in this circumstance.

And any changes in the data require a complete rewrite of the string into the database instead of the much more efficient writing of only the changes. Early editions of the MySQl 5.7 functions also did complete rewrites of JSON data type fields but the engineers quickly sought to go the more efficient route.

The JSON Data Type

MySQL introduced a native JSON datatype in MySQL 5.7. This means that JSON is another data type just like an INT, a REAL, a CHAR, a VARCHAR, or a BLOB. And the JSON data type is designed to hold valid JSON documents.

```
MySQL  localhost:33060+ ssl  json  SQL > CREATE TABLE bar (our_data JSON);
Query OK, 0 rows affected (0.1181 sec)
MySQL  localhost:33060+ ssl  json  SQL > INSERT INTO bar VALUES ('{ "name" : "Bond", "first" : "James", "ID" : "007
" }');
Query OK, 1 row affected (0.0161 sec)
MySQL  localhost:33060+ ssl  json  SQL >
```

```
mysql> CREATE TABLE bar (our_data JSON);

Query OK, 0 rows affected (0.40 sec)

mysql> INSERT INTO bar

       VALUES ('{ "name" : "Bond",

               "first" : "James",

               "ID" : "007" }');
```

Example 2-4 -- Using the JSON data type

The insertion string is the same as in the previous example where the data was stored in a CHAR(250) column.

```
MySQL  localhost:33060+ ssl  json  SQL > SELECT * FROM bar;
+------------------------------------------+
| our_data                                 |
+------------------------------------------+
| {"ID": "007", "name": "Bond", "first": "James"} |
+------------------------------------------+
1 row in set (0.0008 sec)
MySQL  localhost:33060+ ssl  json  SQL >
```

```
mysql> SELECT * FROM bar;

+--------------------------------------------------+
| our_data                                         |
+--------------------------------------------------+
| {"ID": "007", "name": "Bond", "first": "James"}  |
+--------------------------------------------------+

1 row in set (0.00 sec)


mysql>
```

Example 2-5 Selecting JSON data from a JSON data type column

Notice the order of the returned data. The ID column is now first instead of last. The MySQL server stores JSON data in a binary format optimized for quick searches which may cause the keys to come back in a different order than they were entered. Why is this?

The server first checks to make sure the document is in a valid JSON format (if not, it will return an error). Then the data is stored in a special internal format optimized for quick look up by keys or array index position. Think of it like a B-Tree or B+-Tree like used by MySQL for indexes within a binary search when the keys have to be set up in alphabetical order to allow for fast binary style searches to retrieve the data as the value does not need be parsed from a text representation. The binary format is structured so that the server can look up sub-objects or nested values directly by key or array index without having to read all of the values that are preceding or following in the document. This may change the order of the keys when the data is stored.

Chapter 3

Finding the Path

MySQL 5.7 introduced the native JSON data type. So like an Integer, Real, Date, or CHAR, there is a datatype JSON formatted data. The server makes sure this data is in a valid JSON format and organizes the data for faster searching. If the document is not in a valid JSON format the server will not accept it and will report it as an error.

The JSON document is divided up into keys and values. The values can also be made up of a deeper set of keys and values. These various keys and values are broken up into the component parts and provides the way or *a path* to navigate through the document. Much of MySQL's JSON path expression work was heavily influenced by Facebooks' DocStore project.

The path to values depends on being able to understand the structure of the document with its keys and values. Some documents can get quite complicated but this chapter will use a fairly simple dataset and its JSON formatted data.

Several of the MySQL supplied JSON functions require a path expression in order to specify unique elements in a JSON document. A path consists of the scope of the path (the outer braces or brackets, followed by one or more path legs made up of the key/values. The MySQL JSON functions are built with the idea that the scope is always the document being searched or otherwise operated on and represented by a leading **$** character. Path legs can be specified using period characters (.). Cells in arrays are represented by **[N],** where N is a non-negative integer, so N must be zero or larger. And remember the first item in that array is at position 0 not position 1. The names of keys must be double-quoted strings.

Examining the world_x Data

MySQL has been using the **world** database for a very long time in their documentation, instructional materials, and other materials. The **world_x** database was created from that data for use with the Document Store and X Devapi materials for the same purpose. It is also a very good set of data for showing the use of MySQL's JSON functions. The *city*, *country*, and *countrylanguages* tables between the two databases are the same but **world_x** has a new table named *countryinfo*.

```
 MySQL  localhost:33060+ ssl  world_x  SQL > USE world_x;
Default schema set to `world_x`.
Fetching table and column names from `world_x` for auto-completion... Press ^C to stop.
 MySQL  localhost:33060+ ssl  world_x  SQL > DESCRIBE countryinfo;
+--------------+---------------+------+-----+---------+-------------------+
| Field        | Type          | Null | Key | Default | Extra             |
+--------------+---------------+------+-----+---------+-------------------+
| doc          | json          | YES  |     | NULL    |                   |
| _id          | varbinary(32) | NO   | PRI | NULL    | STORED GENERATED  |
| _json_schema | json          | YES  |     | NULL    | VIRTUAL GENERATED |
+--------------+---------------+------+-----+---------+-------------------+
3 rows in set (0.0032 sec)
 MySQL  localhost:33060+ ssl  world_x  SQL >
```

mysql> **USE world_x;**

Database changed

mysql> **DESCRIBE countryinfo;**

```
+-------+-------------+------+-----+---------+-----------------+
| Field | Type        | Null | Key | Default | Extra           |
+-------+-------------+------+-----+---------+-----------------+
| doc   | json        | YES  |     | NULL    |                 |
| _id   | varchar(32) | NO   | PRI | NULL    | STORED GENERATED |
+-------+-------------+------+-----+---------+-----------------+
2 rows in set (0.00 sec)

mysql>
```

Example 3 -1 Examining the *countryinfo* collection structure

This new table has two columns with one being of type JSON. The second column will be ignored until Chapter 7 on Generated Columns. And these two columns will make a little more sense on the later chapters on the MySQL Document Store. For now, please concentrate on the JDON column named **doc**. Note that this name will be used over and over again for JSON columns and hopefully this will not cause confusion (and you can name JSON columns something else at your discretion.

```
MySQL  localhost:33060+ ssl  world_x  SQL > SELECT doc FROM countryinfo WHERE _id = 'USA'\G
*************************** 1. row ***************************
doc: {"GNP": 8510700, "_id": "USA", "Name": "United States", "IndepYear": 1776, "geography": {"Region": "North A
ca", "Continent": "North America", "SurfaceArea": 9363520}, "government": {"HeadOfState": "George W. Bush", "Gov
entForm": "Federal Republic"}, "demographics": {"Population": 278357000, "LifeExpectancy": 77.0999984741211}}
1 row in set (0.0008 sec)
MySQL  localhost:33060+ ssl  world_x  SQL >
```

```
mysql> SELECT doc
       FROM countryinfo
       WHERE _id='USA';
| doc
| {"GNP": 8510700, "_id": "USA", "Name": "United States",
"IndepYear": 1776, "geography": {"Region": "North America",
```

```
"Continent": "North America", "SurfaceArea": 9363520},
"government": {"HeadOfState": "George W. Bush",
"GovernmentForm": "Federal Republic"}, "demographics":
{"Population": 278357000, "LifeExpectancy":
77.0999984741211}} |

1 row in set (0.00 sec)

mysql>
```

**Example 3-2 Selecting one record from the *countryinfo*
collections, using the _id of USA. Please note that some
versions of this data will not return data as the *_id* field had
a value changed from 'USA' to '00005de917d800000000000000df'.
Please ignore this error for now and follow along with the
examples below.**

Examining one record, here the record with the **_id** field
equal to 'USA', returns one example record. Since it is all
enclosed in braces '{' and '}', it is obvious that the output is
a JSON object. The various items can be read however it is hard
to see the levels and relationships. The earlier bragging about
the ease of JSON on the human eye seems to be simply a boast at
this time. Luckily there is a function to improve readability.

```
 MySQL  localhost:33060+ ssl  world_x  SQL > SELECT JSON_PRETTY(doc)
                                        -> FROM countryinfo
                                        -> WHERE _id = "USA"\G
*************************** 1. row ***************************
JSON_PRETTY(doc): {
  "GNP": 8510700,
  "_id": "USA",
  "Name": "United States",
  "IndepYear": 1776,
  "geography": {
    "Region": "North America",
    "Continent": "North America",
    "SurfaceArea": 9363520
  },
  "government": {
    "HeadOfState": "George W. Bush",
    "GovernmentForm": "Federal Republic"
  },
  "demographics": {
    "Population": 278357000,
    "LifeExpectancy": 77.0999984741211
  }
}
1 row in set (0.0005 sec)
 MySQL  localhost:33060+ ssl  world_x  SQL >
```

```
mysql> SELECT JSON_PRETTY(doc)
       FROM countryinfo
       WHERE _id='USA';
| {
  "GNP": 8510700,
  "_id": "USA",
  "Name": "United States",
  "IndepYear": 1776,
  "geography": {
    "Region": "North America",
    "Continent": "North America",
    "SurfaceArea": 9363520
  },
```

```
  "government": {
    "HeadOfState": "George W. Bush",
    "GovernmentForm": "Federal Republic"
  },
  "demographics": {
    "Population": 278357000,
    "LifeExpectancy": 77.0999984741211
  }
} |
```

Example 3-3 Using the JSON_PRETTY function

The **JSON_PRETTY()** function was introduced with MySQL 8 and is used to improve readability of the output. It is similar to pretty-printing found in PHP and other programming languages. It displays each element on its one line and indents by an additional level from the parent. Two spaces are prepended for each level of indentation, and note that a comma (,) is printed before a newline separating elements.

Besides cleaning up the output, **JSON_PRETTY()** helps give the casual observer an easier to understand view of the data. Now it becomes easier to examine the data -- Objects and arrays -- and see the structure. Now it is much easier to see the keys and the values and the path on how they are arranged. But **JSON_PRETTY()** can not work miracles and heavily embedded data may be made only marginally more legible.

Seeing the Keys

There is another function **JSON_KEYS()** that will display the individual keys.

```
MySQL  localhost:33060+ ssl  world_x  SQL > SELECT JSON_KEYS(doc)
                                        -> FROM countryinfo
                                        -> WHERE _id='USA'\G
*************************** 1. row ***************************
JSON_KEYS(doc): ["GNP", "_id", "Name", "IndepYear", "geography", "government", "demographics"]
1 row in set (0.0009 sec)
MySQL  localhost:33060+ ssl  world_x  SQL >
```

```
mysql> SELECT JSON_KEYS(doc)
       FROM countryinfo
       WHERE _id='USA';
+--------------------------------------------------------------------------------+
| JSON_KEYS(doc)                                                                 |
+--------------------------------------------------------------------------------+
| ["GNP", "_id", "Name", "IndepYear", "geography", "government", "demographics"] |
+--------------------------------------------------------------------------------+
1 row in set (0.00 sec)

mysql>
```

Example 3-4 Using the JSON_KEYS function

You can also wrap **JSON_PRETTY()** around **JSON_KEYS()** to improve readability. Generally you can wrap one function within other functions but it is advisable to double check if the combination makes logical sense, i.e. not trying to aggregate arrays of objects, and has purpose. You will notice extensive use of this function throughout this book.

```
MySQL  localhost:33060+ ssl  world_x  SQL > SELECT JSON_PRETTY(JSON_KEYS(doc))
                                        -> FROM countryinfo
                                        -> WHERE _id='USA'\G
*************************** 1. row ***************************
JSON_PRETTY(JSON_KEYS(doc)): [
  "GNP",
  "_id",
  "Name",
  "IndepYear",
  "geography",
  "government",
  "demographics"
]
1 row in set (0.0009 sec)
MySQL  localhost:33060+ ssl  world_x  SQL >
```

mysql> **SELECT JSON_PRETTY(JSON_KEYS(doc))**

      FROM countryinfo

      WHERE _id='USA';

| JSON_PRETTY(JSON_KEYS(doc))

|

| [

  "GNP",

  "_id",

  "Name",

  "IndepYear",

  "geography",

  "government",

  "demographics"

] |

1 row in set (0.00 sec)

Example 3-5 Using JSON_PRETTY and JSON_KEYS together

Note that only the top level keys are being displayed. So "geography" is displayed but not the sub items of "region", "Continent", or "SurfaceArea".

Path

To get the "geography" information we need to specify the path. After naming the column, there is a second argument for the path to search under the top level. Using the dollar sign ($) to represent the current document (remember the JSON column is a JSON document) we can specify the keys under the geography key.

```
MySQL  localhost:33060+ ssl  world_x  SQL > SELECT JSON_KEYS(doc,"$.geography")
                                        -> FROM countryinfo
                                        -> WHERE _id='USA'\G
*************************** 1. row ***************************
JSON_KEYS(doc,"$.geography"): ["Region", "Continent", "SurfaceArea"]
1 row in set (0.0009 sec)
MySQL  localhost:33060+ ssl  world_x  SQL >
```

```
mysql> SELECT JSON_KEYS(doc,"$.geography")
       FROM countryinfo
       WHERE _id='USA';
+-------------------------------------+
| JSON_KEYS(doc,"$.geography")         |
+-------------------------------------+
| ["Region", "Continent", "SurfaceArea"] |
+-------------------------------------+
1 row in set (0.00 sec)

mysql>
```

Example 3-6 Selecting second level keys

Please note that **JSON_KEYS(doc,"$")** returns the top level keys. The second through nth level keys must be post pended to the **$** to be reached.

Digging Deeper

But how can you dig down further in the document to get more information? First thing, the scope of what the function is acting on is the current document, also known as **$**. The path is made up of one or more legs in the document. These legs can be made up of arrays and objects, the keys and values. To get all the information stored with the "geography" key it is necessary to specify "$.geography".

```
MySQL  localhost:33060+ ssl  world_x  SQL > SELECT JSON_EXTRACT(doc,"$.geography")
                            -> FROM countryinfo
                            -> WHERE _id='USA'\G
*************************** 1. row ***************************
JSON_EXTRACT(doc,"$.geography"): {"Region": "North America", "Continent": "North America", "SurfaceArea": 9363520}
1 row in set (0.0008 sec)
MySQL  localhost:33060+ ssl  world_x  SQL >
```

```
mysql> SELECT JSON_EXTRACT(doc,"$.geography")
       FROM countryinfo
       WHERE _id='USA';
+-----------------------------------------------------------------------------------+
| JSON_EXTRACT(doc,"$.geography")                                                   |
+-----------------------------------------------------------------------------------+
| {"Region": "North America", "Continent": "North America", "SurfaceArea": 9363520} |
+-----------------------------------------------------------------------------------+
```

Example 3-7 Digging into second level keys

This provides all the key/value pairs under the *geography* sub path for this document.

But what if it is needed to further go down the *geography* sub path. For instance, what if the *Region* section of the *sub path* is the desired information? Then the sub path and the key of the desired pair needs to be specified.

```
mysql> SELECT JSON_EXTRACT(doc,"$.geography.Region")
       FROM countryinfo
       WHERE _id='USA';
+----------------------------------------+
| JSON_EXTRACT(doc,"$.geography.Region") |
+----------------------------------------+
| "North America"                        |
+----------------------------------------+
1 row in set (0.00 sec)
```

Example 3-8 Digging deeper using the keys to explore the geography.Region values

In Example 3-8 the full path is *$.geography.Region* is provided to retrieve the desired information. And yes it is case sensitive.

In cases the final sub path is a certain value but the other high level keys are unknown are a good case for using a wildcard. The asterisk (*) can be used as a wild card but note that it would pick up all final keys with the name "Region".

```
MySQL  localhost:33060+ ssl  world_x  SQL > SELECT JSON_EXTRACT(doc,"$.*.Region")
                                      ->          FROM countryinfo
                                      ->     WHERE _id='USA';
+-------------------------------+
| JSON_EXTRACT(doc,"$.*.Region") |
+-------------------------------+
| ["North America"]             |
+-------------------------------+
1 row in set (0.0006 sec)
MySQL  localhost:33060+ ssl  world_x  SQL >
```

```
mysql> SELECT JSON_EXTRACT(doc,"$.*.Region")
       FROM countryinfo
       WHERE _id='USA';
       +-------------------------------+
       | JSON_EXTRACT(doc,"$.*.Region") |
       +-------------------------------+
       | ["North America"]             |
       +-------------------------------+
       1 row in set (0.00 sec)
```

Example 3-9 Using a wildcard to find Region data but without having to specify the other keys in the document path.

```
Chapter 4
```

Finding and Getting Data

This chapter deals with the many functions for finding and
retrieving data from the MySQL Server. There are often many
ways to accomplish the same task so seek out the more efficient
ways of doing things.

All Keys

Earlier the **JSON_KEYS()** function was introduced. This
function returns the top level of a JSON object as an array.
Without the optional path it will provide the top level keys.
With the optional path it provides the top level keys from that
path.

Format: **JSON_KEYS(json_doc[, path])**

```
MySQL  localhost:33060+ ssl  world_x  SQL > SELECT JSON_KEYS(doc)
                                    ->     FROM countryinfo
                                    ->     WHERE _id = 'USA';
+-----------------------------------------------------------------------------+
| JSON_KEYS(doc)                                                              |
+-----------------------------------------------------------------------------+
| ["GNP", "_id", "Name", "IndepYear", "geography", "government", "demographics"] |
+-----------------------------------------------------------------------------+
1 row in set (0.0006 sec)
MySQL  localhost:33060+ ssl  world_x  SQL >
```

```
mysql> SELECT JSON_KEYS(doc)
       FROM countryinfo
       WHERE _id = 'USA';
+-----------------------------------------------------------------------------+
| JSON_KEYS(doc)                                                              |
+-----------------------------------------------------------------------------+
| ["GNP", "_id", "Name", "IndepYear", "geography", "government", "demographics"] |
+-----------------------------------------------------------------------------+
1 row in set (0.00 sec)
```

Example 4-1 - JSON_KEYS with top level of JSON document.

The path option allows access to the data stored on the path. In the example below the *geography* path is examined.

```
MySQL  localhost:33060+ ssl  world_x  SQL > SELECT JSON_KEYS(doc,"$.geography")
                                        -> FROM countryinfo
                                        -> WHERE _id = 'USA';
+---------------------------------------+
| JSON_KEYS(doc,"$.geography")           |
+---------------------------------------+
| ["Region", "Continent", "SurfaceArea"] |
+---------------------------------------+
1 row in set (0.0006 sec)
MySQL  localhost:33060+ ssl  world_x  SQL >
```

```
mysql> SELECT JSON_KEYS(doc,"$.geography")
       FROM countryinfo
       WHERE _id = 'USA';
+---------------------------------------+
| JSON_KEYS(doc,"$.geography")           |
+---------------------------------------+
| ["Region", "Continent", "SurfaceArea"] |
+---------------------------------------+
1 row in set (0.00 sec)

mysql>
```

Example 4-2 - JSON_KEYS with optional key to use as as top level for reporting

Also refer to Examples 3-8 and 3-9 for specifying deeper level keys and wildcard characters with a document.

Is The Key There?

Suppose you have a valid JSON document in a column of row in a table and you need to search for a certain key in that data. Or for all of a certain key in the data (second phone number, additional email addresses, and the like). **JSON_CONTAINS_PATH** uses the second argument, either a **ONE** or an **ALL**, to determine if it will return after finding just the first occurrence (or returning all) from the path given as the third (and later) arguments.

Format: **JSON_CONTAINS_PATH(json_doc, one_or_all, path[, path] ...)**

```
mysql> SELECT JSON_CONTAINS_PATH(doc,"ONE","$.geography")
       FROM countryinfo
       WHERE _id='USA';
+---------------------------------------------+
| JSON_CONTAINS_PATH(doc,"ONE","$.geography") |
+---------------------------------------------+
|                                           1 |
+---------------------------------------------+
1 row in set (0.00 sec)

mysql>
```

Example 4-3 - JSON_CONTAINS_PATH used to search for key 'geography'

In the above example there is a match in the specific document to the key *geography* and the server returns a 1. A failure to match will return a 0.

Is the Path There?

JSON_CONTAINS_PATH() returns a **1** (true) if the desired key is in the document. In the example above there is a "geography" key so a **1** is returned. A **0** is returned if the document/columns does not have the desired key. The 'logical' functions that perform tests will return zeros or ones, not the values underneath.

Multiple keys can be searched for in one statement. The following example is looking for both the **geography** and **government** keys. So both keys must be present for the server to return a 1.

Format: **JSON_CONTAINS_PATH(json_doc, one_or_all, path[, path] ...)**

```
MySQL  localhost:33060+ ssl  world_x  SQL  > SELECT JSON_CONTAINS_PATH(doc,"ONE","$.geography","$.government")
                                         -> FROM countryinfo
                                         -> WHERE _id='USA'\G
*************************** 1. row ***************************
JSON_CONTAINS_PATH(doc,"ONE","$.geography","$.government"): 1
1 row in set (0.0009 sec)
MySQL  localhost:33060+ ssl  world_x  SQL  >
```

mysql> **SELECT**

JSON_CONTAINS_PATH(doc,"ONE","$.geography","$.government")

FROM countryinfo

WHERE _id='USA';

```
+-----------------------------------------------------------
--+
|
JSON_CONTAINS_PATH(doc,"ONE","$.geography","$.government")
|
+-----------------------------------------------------------
--+
|
1 |
+-----------------------------------------------------------
--+
1 row in set (0.00 sec)
```

mysql>

Example 4-4 -- Searching for 'geography' *and* **'government'**
keys in the data.

The second argument this functions is either **ONE** or **ALL**.
Use **ONE** for when one key exists at least once in the path. And
use **ALL** when you desire to have all keys present.

```
MySQL  localhost:33060+ ssl  world_x  SQL > SELECT JSON_CONTAINS_PATH(doc,"ONE","$.geography","$.governmentx")
                                     -> FROM countryinfo
                                     -> WHERE _id='USA'\G
*************************** 1. row ***************************
JSON_CONTAINS_PATH(doc,"ONE","$.geography","$.governmentx"): 1
1 row in set (0.0012 sec)
MySQL  localhost:33060+ ssl  world_x  SQL >
```

mysql> **SELECT**
JSON_CONTAINS_PATH(doc,"ALL","$.geography","$.governmentx")
FROM countryinfo
WHERE _id='USA';

```
+-------------------------------------------------------------+
| JSON_CONTAINS_PATH(doc,"ALL","$.geography","$.governmentx") |
+-------------------------------------------------------------+
|                                                           0 |
+-------------------------------------------------------------+
1 row in set (0.00 sec)
```

mysql>

Example 4-5 -- Failure using JSON_CONTAINS path, indicated by the 0 because there is no 'governmentx' key within the data.

In the above example a **0** is returned; there is a "geography" key in the document/column but not a "governmentx". So the server reports no match.

Is the Value There

JSON_CONTAINS() is used to see if the value of specified key matches a specified value. It is an equivalency function: does A equal B?

Format: **JSON_CONTAINS(json_doc, val[, path])**

```
MySQL  localhost:33060+ ssl  world_x  SQL > SELECT JSON_CONTAINS(doc,"1776","$.IndepYear")
                                        -> FROM countryinfo
                                        -> WHERE _id='USA'\G
*************************** 1. row ***************************
JSON_CONTAINS(doc,"1776","$.IndepYear"): 1
1 row in set (0.0010 sec)
MySQL  localhost:33060+ ssl  world_x  SQL >
```

```
mysql> SELECT JSON_CONTAINS(doc,"1776","$.IndepYear")
       FROM countryinfo
       WHERE _id='USA';
+-----------------------------------------+
| JSON_CONTAINS(doc,"1776","$.IndepYear") |
+-----------------------------------------+
|                                       1 |
+-----------------------------------------+
1 row in set (0.00 sec)

mysql>
```

Example 4-6 - Using JSON_CONTAINS to determine if the value of IndepYear of this record equals 1776.

In the above example the *IndepYear* does match the value 1776 for the document with the *_id* value equal to USA.

JSON_SEARCH() returns the position or key of a value. Previous functions provided the value given a key.

```
MySQL  localhost:33060+ ssl  world_x  SQL > SELECT JSON_SEARCH(doc,"ONE", "United States")
                                         -> FROM countryinfo
                                         -> WHERE _id='USA'\G
*************************** 1. row ***************************
JSON_SEARCH(doc,"ONE", "United States"): "$.Name"
1 row in set (0.0010 sec)
MySQL  localhost:33060+ ssl  world_x  SQL >
```

```
mysql> SELECT JSON_SEARCH(doc,"ONE", "United States")
       FROM countryinfo
       WHERE _id='usa';
+-----------------------------------------+
| JSON_SEARCH(doc,"ONE", "United States") |
+-----------------------------------------+
| "$.Name"                                |
+-----------------------------------------+
1 row in set (0.00 sec)

mysql>
```

Example 4-7 – Which key in the document path has the value of 'United States'?

This function will also check the full path and return matching keys. Note that this is searching on the value to return the key. Previous examples were looking for the values given a key while JSON_SEARCH returns keys given values. This function will provide the full path of the key for the given value.

```
MySQL  localhost:33060+ ssl  world_x  SQL > SELECT JSON_SEARCH(doc,"ONE", "North America")
                                         -> FROM countryinfo
                                         -> WHERE _id='USA'\G
*************************** 1. row ***************************
JSON_SEARCH(doc,"ONE", "North America"): "$.geography.Region"
1 row in set (0.0012 sec)
MySQL  localhost:33060+ ssl  world_x  SQL >
```

```
mysql> SELECT JSON_SEARCH(doc,"ONE", "North America")
       FROM countryinfo
       WHERE _id='usa';
+----------------------------------------+
| JSON_SEARCH(doc,"ONE", "North America") |
+----------------------------------------+
| "$.geography.Region"                   |
+----------------------------------------+
1 row in set (0.00 sec)

mysql>
```

Example 4-8 - Where is North America in this JSON document? JSON_SEARCH provides a way to find the key given a value.

Searching for a Boolean Value

One thing to note is that **JSON_SEARCH()** does not let you directly search for a boolean value. If you need to find a 'true' or 'false' value you can augment the capabilities of JSON_EXTRACT() with the INSTR() function to accomplish this.

```
MySQL  localhost:33060+ ssl  book  SQL > CREATE TABLE booltest (id INT UNSIGNED, doc JSON);
Query OK, 0 rows affected (0.1156 sec)
MySQL  localhost:33060+ ssl  book  SQL > INSERT INTO booltest
                                    ->     VALUES (1, '{"finished" : "true" }');
Query OK, 1 row affected (0.0207 sec)
MySQL  localhost:33060+ ssl  book  SQL > INSERT INTO booltest
                                    ->     VALUES (99, '{  "finished" : "true" }');
Query OK, 1 row affected (0.0179 sec)
MySQL  localhost:33060+ ssl  book  SQL > INSERT INTO booltest
                                    ->     VALUES (94, '{  "finished" : "false" }');
Query OK, 1 row affected (0.0188 sec)
MySQL  localhost:33060+ ssl  book  SQL > SELECT id
                                    -> FROM booltest
                                    -> WHERE INSTR(JSON_EXTRACT(doc, "$.finished"), 'true')\g
+----+
| id |
+----+
|  1 |
| 99 |
+----+
2 rows in set (0.0006 sec)
```

mysql> **CREATE TABLE booltest (id INT UNSIGNED, doc JSON);**

Query OK, 0 rows affected (0.0644 sec)

mysql> **INSERT INTO booltest**

      VALUES (1, '{"finished" : "true" }');

Query OK, 1 row affected (0.0124 sec)

mysql> **INSERT INTO booltest**

      VALUES (99, '{ "finished" : "true" }');

Query OK, 1 row affected (0.0054 sec)

mysql> **INSERT INTO booltest**

      VALUES (94, '{ "finished" : "false" }');

Query OK, 1 row affected (0.0048 sec)

mysql> **SELECT id**

      FROM booltest

      WHERE

       INSTR(JSON_EXTRACT(doc, "$.finished"), 'true');

```
+----+
| id |
+----+
|  1 |
| 99 |
```

```
+----+
```
2 rows in set (0.0013 sec)

Example 4-9 -- Finding a boolean value when JSON_SEARCH() can not return the proper answer.

Multi-Value Indexes

Multi-value indexes were added in MySQL 8.0.17 and is a great benefit for indexing each member of a JSON array. Previously indexes were limited to one index entry per row of data. But in cases where a person may have multiple phone numbers or the document for a customer order contains many stock keeping unit numbers, there is a lot of benefit that can be had from Multi-value indexes.

The functions **MEMBER OF, JSON_CONTAINS()**, and **JSON_OVERLAP()** are designed to take advantage of these Multi-valued indexes but are not solely dependent on them. See the chapter on Multi-value indexes for more information on creating and using them. These three functions have the ability to take advantage of the Multi-valued indexes which can greatly increase the performance of a query.

The **MEMBER OF** function tests to see if a value is a member of a JSON array. It will return 1 or true if the value is an element of the array.

Format: **value** MEMBER OF (**json_array**)

```
MySQL  localhost:33060+ ssl  book  SQL > SELECT 'Joe' MEMBER OF ('["Joe","Betty","Hakeem"]');
+----------------------------------------------+
| 'Joe' MEMBER OF ('["Joe","Betty","Hakeem"]') |
+----------------------------------------------+
|                                            1 |
+----------------------------------------------+
1 row in set (0.0003 sec)
```

```
> SELECT 'Joe' MEMBER OF ('["Joe","Betty","Hakeem"]');

+----------------------------------------------+
| 'Joe' MEMBER OF ('["Joe","Betty","Hakeem"]') |
+----------------------------------------------+
|                                            1 |
+----------------------------------------------+
1 row in set (0.0005 sec)
```

Example 4-10 -- Using MEMBER OF to determine if `Joe' is part of the group provided.

And it also works well on arrays of number or mixed numbers and strings.

```
MySQL  localhost:33060+ ssl  book  SQL > SELECT 5
                              -> MEMBER OF ('[1, 3, 5, 7, 9, 11]');
+--------------------------------------+
| 5
MEMBER OF ('[1, 3, 5, 7, 9, 11]') |
+--------------------------------------+
|                                    1 |
+--------------------------------------+
1 row in set (0.0007 sec)
MySQL  localhost:33060+ ssl  book  SQL > SELECT 5
                              -> MEMBER OF
                              -> ('[1, 3, 5, "Fred", 7, 9, "Lenka", 11]');
+---------------------------------------------+
| 5
MEMBER OF
('[1, 3, 5, "Fred", 7, 9, "Lenka", 11]') |
+---------------------------------------------+
|                                           1 |
+---------------------------------------------+
1 row in set (0.0005 sec)
MySQL  localhost:33060+ ssl  book  SQL >
```

```
mysql> SELECT 5 MEMBER OF ('[1, 3, 5, 7, 9, 11]');
+--------------------------------------+
```

```
| 5 MEMBER OF ('[1, 3, 5, 7, 9, 11]') |
+-------------------------------------+
|                                   1 |
+-------------------------------------+
1 row in set (0.0008 sec)

Smysql> SELECT 5 MEMBER OF
     ('[1, 3, 5, "Fred", 7, 9, "Lenka", 11]');
+------------------------------------------------------+
| 5 MEMBER OF ('[1, 3, 5, "Fred", 7, 9, "Lenka", 11]') |
+------------------------------------------------------+
|                                                    1 |
+------------------------------------------------------+
1 row in set (0.0006 sec)
```

Example 4-11 -- Using MEMBER OF to check integer values and mixed integers and strings

JSON_CONTAINS() Indicates by returning 1 or 0 whether a given candidate JSON document is contained within a target JSON document, or — if a path argument was supplied — whether the candidate is found at a specific path within the target.

Format: **JSON_CONTAINS(target, candidate[, path])**

```
mysql> SELECT JSON_CONTAINS('{"Moe": 1, "Larry":
2}','{"Moe": 1}');
+----------------------------------------------------+
| JSON_CONTAINS('{"Moe": 1, "Larry": 2}','{"Moe": 1}') |
+----------------------------------------------------+
|                                                  1 |
+----------------------------------------------------+
1 row in set (0.0016 sec)
```

Example 4-12 - Using JSON_CONTAINS() to determine if the target document contains the candidate document

```
MySQL  localhost:33060+ ssl  book  SQL > SELECT JSON_CONTAINS('{"Moe": 7, "Larry": 2}',
                                  ->                           '7','$.Moe');
+----------------------------------------------------------------+
| JSON_CONTAINS('{"Moe": 7, "Larry": 2}',
                          '7','$.Moe') |
+----------------------------------------------------------------+
|                                                              1 |
+----------------------------------------------------------------+
1 row in set (0.0005 sec)
MySQL  localhost:33060+ ssl  book  SQL >
```

```
mysql> SELECT JSON_CONTAINS('{"Moe": 7, "Larry": 2}',
                            '7','$.Moe');
+-------------------------------------------------------+
| JSON_CONTAINS('{"Moe": 7, "Larry": 2}','1','$.Moe') |
+-------------------------------------------------------+
|                                                   1 |
+-------------------------------------------------------+
```

Example 4-13 -- Using JSON_CONTAINS() with the path option to determine if the `$.Moe object has a value of 7.

Format: **JSON_OVERLAPS(document1, document2)**

This function compares two JSON documents and returns 1 or true if it has any key/value pairs or array elements in common.

```
MySQL  localhost:33060+ ssl  book  SQL > SELECT JSON_OVERLAPS("[1,3,5,7]","[2,3,4,5]");
+--------------------------------------+
| JSON_OVERLAPS("[1,3,5,7]","[2,3,4,5]") |
+--------------------------------------+
|                                    1 |
+--------------------------------------+
1 row in set (0.0003 sec)
MySQL  localhost:33060+ ssl  book  SQL >
```

45

```
mysql> SELECT JSON_OVERLAPS("[1,3,5,7]","[2,3,4,5]");
+----------------------------------------+
| JSON_OVERLAPS("[1,3,5,7]","[2,3,4,5]") |
+----------------------------------------+
|                                      1 |
+----------------------------------------+
1 row in set (0.00 sec)
```

Example 4 - 14 - JSON_OVERLAPS() compares documents to test if two documents have data in common

```
MySQL  localhost:33060+ ssl  book  SQL > SELECT JSON_OVERLAPS("[1,3,5,7]","[2,4,6]"
+--------------------------------------+
| JSON_OVERLAPS("[1,3,5,7]","[2,4,6]") |
+--------------------------------------+
|                                    0 |
+--------------------------------------+
1 row in set (0.0007 sec)
MySQL  localhost:33060+ ssl  book  SQL >
```

```
mysql> SELECT JSON_OVERLAPS("[1,3,5,7]","[2,4,6]");
+--------------------------------------+
| JSON_OVERLAPS("[1,3,5,7]","[2,4,6]") |
+--------------------------------------+
|                                    0 |
+--------------------------------------+
    1 row in set (0.00 sec)
```

Example 4-15 JSON_OVERLAPS() returns zero or false if there is nothing in common between the two documents

The Difference between JSON_CONTAINS() and JSON_OVERLAPS()

So what is the difference between these two functions? **JSON_CONTAINS()** requires ALL elements of the array searched for to be present while **JSON_OVERLAPS()** looks for any matches. So think **JSON_CONTAINS()** as the AND operation on KEYS while **JSON_OVERLAP()** is the OR operator.

```
MySQL  localhost:33060+ ssl  book  SQL > SELECT JSON_OVERLAPS("[1,3,5,7]","[1,3,5,9]");
+---------------------------------------+
| JSON_OVERLAPS("[1,3,5,7]","[1,3,5,9]") |
+---------------------------------------+
|                                     1 |
+---------------------------------------+
1 row in set (0.0004 sec)
MySQL  localhost:33060+ ssl  book  SQL > SELECT JSON_CONTAINS("[1,3,5,7]","[1,3,5,9]");
+---------------------------------------+
| JSON_CONTAINS("[1,3,5,7]","[1,3,5,9]") |
+---------------------------------------+
|                                     0 |
+---------------------------------------+
1 row in set (0.0007 sec)
MySQL  localhost:33060+ ssl  book  SQL >
```

```
mysql> SELECT JSON_OVERLAPS("[1,3,5,7]","[1,3,5,9]");
+---------------------------------------+
| JSON_OVERLAPS("[1,3,5,7]","[1,3,5,9]") |
+---------------------------------------+
|                                     1 |
+---------------------------------------+
1 row in set (0.00 sec)


mysql> SELECT JSON_CONTAINS("[1,3,5,7]","[1,3,5,9]");
+---------------------------------------+
| JSON_CONTAINS("[1,3,5,7]","[1,3,5,9]") |
+---------------------------------------+
|                                     0 |
+---------------------------------------+
1 row in set (0.00 sec)
```

> **Example 4-16 -- JSON_OVERLAPS() and
> JSON_CONTAINS() are similar but JSON_OVERLAP() looks
> for any matches like an OR whole JSON_CONTAINS() needs
> all elements to match line an AND**

The example 4-16 shows the difference clearly. In the
top example there is some 'overlap' between the numbers in
the arrays. In the bottom example there is not an exact
match.

JSON_VALUE

MySQL 8.0.21 Added the **JSON_VALUE()** function, which simplifies creating indexes on JSON columns. A call to **JSON_VALUE(json_doc, path RETURNING type)** is equivalent to calling **CAST(JSON_UNQUOTE(JSON_EXTRACT(json_doc, path)) AS type)**, where json_doc is a JSON document, path is a JSON path expression pointing to a single value within the document, and type is a data type compatible with **CAST()**. RETURNING type is optional; if no return type is specified, **JSON_VALUE()** returns VARCHAR(512). **JSON_VALUE()** also supports ON EMPTY and ON ERROR clauses similar to those used with **JSON_TABLE()**.

The following example shows the use of **JSON_VALUE()** to cast the value 77.0999984741211 as a **DECIMAL(4.2)** type which returns a value of 77.10.

```
MySQL  localhost:33060+ ssl  world_x  SQL > SELECT
                                        -> JSON_EXTRACT(doc,"$.demographics.LifeExpectancy") as raw,
                                        -> JSON_VALUE(doc,"$.demographics.LifeExpectancy" RETURNING DECIMAL(4,2)) as trimmed
                                        -> FROM countryinfo
                                        -> WHERE _id='USA';
+-------------------+---------+
| raw               | trimmed |
+-------------------+---------+
| 77.0999984741211  |   77.10 |
+-------------------+---------+
1 row in set (0.0005 sec)
MySQL  localhost:33060+ ssl  world_x  SQL >
```

```
mysql> SELECT
JSON_EXTRACT(doc,"$.demographics.LifeExpectancy") as raw,
JSON_VALUE(doc,"$.demographics.LifeExpectancy" RETURNING
DECIMAL(4,2)) as trimmed
FROM countryinfo
WHERE _id='USA';
```

Example 4-17 -- Using JSON_VALUE() to cast a value of type DECIMAL()

The original MySQl Worklog for **JSON_VALUE()** (WL #12228 for the curious) states the original goal was to ease the creation of indexes by extracting a scalar value at the specified path and return it as the specified type. The **JSON_VALUE()** function's default return type is a **VARCHAR(512)** which is much handier than the **BLOB** default returned by **JSON_UNQUOTE()** for creating indexes. You can create indexes on a JSON column using **JSON_VALUE()** as shown here:

```
MySQL  localhost:33060+ ssl  world_x  SQL > CREATE TABLE inventory(
                             ->     items JSON,
                             -> INDEX i3 ( (JSON_VALUE(items, '$.quantity'
                             -> RETURNING UNSIGNED)) )
                             -> );
Query OK, 0 rows affected (0.1181 sec)
MySQL  localhost:33060+ ssl  world_x  SQL >
```

```
CREATE TABLE inventory(
        items JSON,
        INDEX i3 ( (JSON_VALUE(items, '$.quantity'
             RETURNING UNSIGNED)) )
);
```

Example 4-18 -- Using JSON_VALUE() to cast values to the desired types.

Assuming the items column contains values such as '{"name": "hat", "price": "22.95", "quantity": "17"}', you can issue queries, such as the following, that can use these indexes:

```
MySQL  localhost:33060+ ssl  world_x  SQL > SELECT items->"$.price"
                             -> FROM inventory
                             -> WHERE JSON_VALUE(items, '$.name') = "hat";
+------------------+
| items->"$.price" |
+------------------+
| "22.95"          |
+------------------+
1 row in set (0.0007 sec)
MySQL  localhost:33060+ ssl  world_x  SQL >
```

```
SELECT items->"$.price"
FROM inventory
WHERE JSON_VALUE(items, '$.name') = "hat";
```

Example 4-18 -- Here JSON_VALUE() is used to cast the '$.name' value to a VARCHAR(50) before the return value is checked to see if it equals "HAT".

One of the better fits for this type of casting is when you need to better test values. In the following example the price data may be kept in an arbitrary format, possibly reflecting real fractional values such as 100.0123 or similar. Or you may need to get the top x percent values and cast the values as integers to facilitate the calculation.

```
MySQL  localhost:33060+ ssl  world_x  SQL > SELECT *
                                        -> FROM inventory
                                        -> WHERE JSON_VALUE(items, '$.price' RETURNIN
                                        -> DECIMAL(5,2)) <= 100.01;
+----------------------------------------------------------+
| items                                                    |
+----------------------------------------------------------+
| {"name": "hat", "price": "22.95", "quantity": "17"} |
+----------------------------------------------------------+
1 row in set (0.0010 sec)
MySQL  localhost:33060+ ssl  world_x  SQL >
```

SELECT *
FROM inventory
WHERE JSON_VALUE(items, '$.price' RETURNING
        DECIMAL(5,2)) <= 100.01;

Example 4-19 -- Turning values of unknown precision to something more useful.

JSON_VALUE() can also be handy when dealing with missing values. In the following case there is no specified last name which can be handled easily by supplying a value.

```
MySQL  localhost:33060+ ssl  world_x  SQL > SELECT (JSON_VALUE("{ 'first_name' : 'Dave'}",'$.last_name'
                                        -> DEFAULT 'No Last Name' ON ERROR)) as "last name";
+--------------+
| last name    |
+--------------+
| No Last Name |
+--------------+
1 row in set, 1 warning (0.0005 sec)
```

SELECT
(JSON_VALUE("{ 'first_name' : 'Dave'}",'$.last_name'
DEFAULT 'No Last Name' ON ERROR)) as "last name";

Example 4-20 -- JSOON_VALUE() allows specification of default values when data is missing or empty. In this example a missing last_name value generates a 'No Last Name' sting.

CHAPTER 5

Changing Data

Arrays

The JSON standard proclaims that array values shall be of type string, number, object, Boolean or null. Arrays are very handy for storing multiple values and unlike objects do not need to be in pairs. Since MySQL does not have an array data type many have used JSON arrays instead. It helps to remember that arrays are bound by square brackets **[]** while objects are bound by curly braces **{}**.

Format: **JSON_ARRAY([val[, val] ...])**

```
MySQL  localhost:33060+ ssl  json  SQL > CREATE DATABASE testjson; USE testjson;
Query OK, 1 row affected (0.0327 sec)
Default schema set to `testjson`.
Fetching table and column names from `testjson` for auto-completion... Press ^C to stop.
MySQL  localhost:33060+ ssl  testjson  SQL > CREATE TABLE y (x JSON);
Query OK, 0 rows affected (0.0900 sec)
MySQL  localhost:33060+ ssl  testjson  SQL > INSERT INTO y VALUES (JSON_ARRAY('A','B','C'));
Query OK, 1 row affected (0.0158 sec)
MySQL  localhost:33060+ ssl  testjson  SQL >
```

mysql> **CREATE DATABASE testjson; USE testjson;**

Database changed

mysql> **CREATE TABLE y (x JSON);**

Query OK, 0 rows affected (0.05 sec)

mysql> **INSERT INTO y VALUES (JSON_ARRAY('A','B','C'));**

Query OK, 1 row affected (0.01 sec)

```
mysql>
```

Example 5-1 -- Creating a new database and table using the JSON data type

Because it would be messy to adulterate the countryinfo tables, a new database schema and table need to be created. The above creates a new schema named testjson, creates a table named y, and inserts some sample data.

This new array has three items. $[0] is set to 'A', $[1] is set to 'B', and $[2] is set to 'C'. Those used to programming languages that start counting from one need to make a mental note as array elements in JSON documents start with zero.

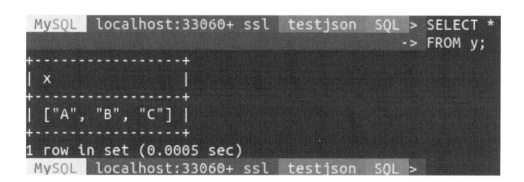

```
mysql> SELECT * FROM y;
+-----------------+
| x               |
+-----------------+
| ["A", "B", "C"] |
```

```
+-----------------+
```

1 row in set (0.00 sec)

Example 5-2 -- Data from the new table

Appending Arrays

    Arrays may need to be augmented and **JSON_ARRAY_APPEND**
appends values to the end of the designated arrays within a JSON
document and then returns the result. It will return a NULL if
any argument is NULL. The server will report an error if the
json_doc argument is not a valid JSON document, any path
argument is not a valid path expression, or it contains a * or
** wildcard. Note that: The path-value pairs are evaluated from
the left to the right. The document that is produced by
evaluating one pair becomes the new value against which the next
pair is evaluated; every new evaluation starts fresh on the
latest version of the document that is being processed. And
remember that the first element in an array is at $[0], and the
second at $[1], and so on.

Format: **JSON_ARRAY_APPEND(json_doc, path, val[, path, val] ...)**

    It is easy to append an asterisk to $[0] as can be seen
below.

```
MySQL  localhost:33060+ ssl  testjson  SQL > UPDATE y SET x=JSON_ARRAY_APPEND(x,"$[0]","*");
Query OK, 1 row affected (0.0147 sec)

Rows matched: 1  Changed: 1  Warnings: 0
 MySQL  localhost:33060+ ssl  testjson  SQL > SELECT * FROM y;
+----------------------+
| x                    |
+----------------------+
| [["A", "*"], "B", "C"] |
+----------------------+
1 row in set (0.0007 sec)
 MySQL  localhost:33060+ ssl  testjson  SQL >
```

mysql> **UPDATE y SET x=JSON_ARRAY_APPEND(x,"$[0]","*");**

Query OK, 1 row affected (0.01 sec)

Rows matched: 1   Changed: 1   Warnings: 0

mysql> **SELECT * FROM y;**

```
+------------------------+
| x                      |
+------------------------+
| [["A", "*"], "B", "C"] |
+------------------------+
```

1 row in set (0.00 sec)

Example 5-3 -- Appending the $[0] value

Now $[0] is set to "A","*". Another way to think about the above change is that $[0] is itself a new array within the previous array.

Note that the data has to exist before it can be appended or it will post-pended.

```
MySQL  localhost:33060+ ssl  testjson  SQL > UPDATE y SET x=JSON_ARRAY_APPEND(x,"$","#");
Query OK, 1 row affected (0.0171 sec)

Rows matched: 1  Changed: 1  Warnings: 0
MySQL  localhost:33060+ ssl  testjson  SQL > SELECT * FROM y;
+-------------------------+
| x                       |
+-------------------------+
| [["A", "*"], "B", "C", "#"] |
+-------------------------+
1 row in set (0.0007 sec)
MySQL  localhost:33060+ ssl  testjson  SQL >
```

mysql> **UPDATE y SET x=JSON_ARRAY_APPEND(x,"$","#");**

Query OK, 1 row affected (0.01 sec)

Rows matched: 1 Changed: 1 Warnings: 0

mysql> **SELECT * FROM y;**

```
+----------------------------+
| x                          |
+----------------------------+
| [["A", "*"], "B", "C", "#"] |
+----------------------------+
```

1 row in set (0.01 sec)

Example 5-4 -- Appending Data

It is also possible to insert multiple values at once. This is
more efficient than sending multiple queries as each query has
to have the user authenticated, syntax check, query plan
generated, and then the query executed. If possible it pays to
do as much on 'one trip' top the server as possible.

```
MySQL  localhost:33060+ ssl  testjson  SQL > UPDATE y      SET x=JSON_ARRAY_APPEND(x,"$[1]","@","$[3]","+");
Query OK, 1 row affected (0.0221 sec)

Rows matched: 1  Changed: 1  Warnings: 0
MySQL  localhost:33060+ ssl  testjson  SQL > SELECT * FROM y;
+-------------------------------------------+
| x                                         |
+-------------------------------------------+
| [["A", "*"], ["B", "@"], "C", ["#", "+"]] |
+-------------------------------------------+
1 row in set (0.0009 sec)
MySQL  localhost:33060+ ssl  testjson  SQL >
```

mysql> **UPDATE y**

    SET x=JSON_ARRAY_APPEND(x,"$[1]","@","$[3]","+");

Query OK, 1 row affected (0.00 sec)

Rows matched: 1 Changed: 1 Warnings: 0

mysql> **SELECT * FROM y;**

```
+-------------------------------------------+
| x                                         |
+-------------------------------------------+
| [["A", "*"], ["B", "@"], "C", ["#", "+"]] |
+-------------------------------------------+
```

1 row in set (0.00 sec)

mysql>

      Example 5-5 -- Updating data

Inserting Into An Array

    JSON_ARRAY_INSERT() is very similar to the previous
JSON_ARRAY_APPEND() but, as the name of the functions states, a
new value is inserted at the desired location. It will return a
NULL if any argument is NULL. The server will report an error if

the json_doc argument is not a valid JSON document, any path argument is not a valid path expression, or it contains a * or ** wildcard. Note that: The path-value pairs are evaluated from the left to the right. The document that is produced by evaluating one pair becomes the new value against which the next pair is evaluated; every new evaluation starts fresh on the latest version of the document that is being processed.

Format: **JSON_ARRAY_INSERT(json_doc, path, val[, path, val] ...)**

```
mysql> UPDATE y SET x=JSON_ARRAY_INSERT(x,"$[0]","&");
Query OK, 1 row affected (0.01 sec)
Rows matched: 1  Changed: 1  Warnings: 0

mysql> SELECT * FROM y;
+------------------------------------------------+
| x                                              |
+------------------------------------------------+
| ["&", ["A", "*"], ["B", "@"], "C", ["#", "+"]] |
+------------------------------------------------+
1 row in set (0.00 sec)
mysql>
```

Example 5-6 Inserting Data

The array changes with $[0] now set to the new value (here an '&') and the others values shifted down. And multiple inserts can be done at the same time.

```
MySQL  localhost:33060+ ssl  testjson  SQL > UPDATE y
                                        -> SET x=JSON_ARRAY_INSERT(x,"$[1]","777","$[3]","999");
Query OK, 1 row affected (0.0135 sec)

Rows matched: 1  Changed: 1  Warnings: 0
MySQL  localhost:33060+ ssl  testjson  SQL > SELECT * FROM y;
+-------------------------------------------------+
| x                                               |
+-------------------------------------------------+
| ["&", "777", ["A", "*"], "999", ["B", "@"], "C", ["#", "+"]] |
+-------------------------------------------------+
1 row in set (0.0009 sec)
MySQL  localhost:33060+ ssl  testjson  SQL >
```

```
mysql> UPDATE y
       SET x=JSON_ARRAY_INSERT(x,"$[1]","777","$[3]","999");
Query OK, 1 row affected (0.01 sec)
Rows matched: 1  Changed: 1  Warnings: 0


mysql> SELECT * FROM y;
+-------------------------------------------------------------+
| x                                                           |
+-------------------------------------------------------------+
| ["&", "777", ["A", "*"], "999", ["B", "@"], "C", ["#", "+"]] |
+-------------------------------------------------------------+
1 row in set (0.00 sec)


mysql>
```

Example 5-7 -- Multiple changes simultaneously made by JSON_ARRAY_INSERT

Again, in general practice it is best with relational databases to make multiple changes with one query over many small changes with multiple queries.

JSON SET, INSERT and Replace

For the next few examples is it best to 'wipe the slate clean' and remove the old data by using truncate and then adding new data. For those unfamiliar with the TRUNCATE command, it removed the data but preserves the underlying table structure.

```
mysql> TRUNCATE y;
Query OK, 0 rows affected (0.02 sec)

mysql> INSERT INTO y
    VALUES('{ "key1" : "value1" }');
Query OK, 1 row affected (0.01 sec)

mysql> SELECT * FROM y;
+--------------------+
| x                  |
```

```
+--------------------+
| {"key1": "value1"} |
+--------------------+
1 row in set (0.00 sec)


mysql>
```

Example 5-8 -- Cleaning the slate of the old array data and starting fresh with an object.

JSON_INSERT

The use of **JSON_INSERT()** is to add values to a JSON document. It is similar to **JSON_SET()** but the set is used with keys and values already existing in the document and **JSON_INSERT()** is adding new data. A path-value pair for an already existing path in the document is ignored and it does not overwrite the existing document value. If a path-value pair for a does not match a path in the document it is ignored and has no effect. The server will report an error if the *json_doc* argument is not a valid JSON document, any path argument is not a valid path expression, or it contains a * or ** wildcard. Note that: The path-value pairs are evaluated from the left to the right.

Format: **JSON_INSERT(json_doc, path, val[, path, val] ...)**

```
mysql> UPDATE y
          SET x = JSON_INSERT(x,'$.key2','value2');
Query OK, 1 row affected (0.01 sec)
Rows matched: 1  Changed: 1  Warnings: 0


mysql> SELECT * FROM y;
+------------------------------------+
| x                                  |
+------------------------------------+
| {"key1": "value1", "key2": "value2"} |
+------------------------------------+
1 row in set (0.00 sec)


mysql>
```

Example 5-9 -- Using JSON_INSERT

Multiple items can be inserted in one statement. The line
is actually read left from right and after each insert the next
step is done with the line re-examined including the new
element.

```
MySQL  localhost:33060+ ssl  testjson  SQL > UPDATE y SET x =
                                          -> JSON_INSERT(x,'$.key1','value1x',"$.key3","value3");
Query OK, 1 row affected (0.0147 sec)

Rows matched: 1  Changed: 1  Warnings: 0
MySQL  localhost:33060+ ssl  testjson  SQL > SELECT * FROM y;
+----------------------------------------------+
| x                                            |
+----------------------------------------------+
| {"key1": "value1", "key2": "value2", "key3": "value3"} |
+----------------------------------------------+
1 row in set (0.0009 sec)
 MySQL  localhost:33060+ ssl  testjson  SQL >
```

mysql> **UPDATE y SET x =**

JSON_INSERT(x,'$.key1','value1x',"$.key3","value3");

Query OK, 1 row affected (0.01 sec)

Rows matched: 1 Changed: 1 Warnings: 0

mysql> SELECT * FROM y;

```
+----------------------------------------------------------+
| x                                                        |
+----------------------------------------------------------+
| {"key1": "value1", "key2": "value2", "key3": "value3"} |
+----------------------------------------------------------+
```

1 row in set (0.00 sec)

mysql>

Example 5-10 -- Multiple inserts with JSON_INSERT

Note that in the above example the query wanted to reset
the values for key1 but failed. Why? Insert is not replaced and
JSON_INSERT() will <u>not</u> replace an existing value. However the
$.key3 information was processed by the server. So half the
above query worked as desired but there was no warning or error

on the half that did not get performed. If you use this
function you need to be very careful as this could lead to major
problems later. It would be very easy to presume key1 has the
value of *value1x* in this case when it does not. And thus
database administrators and developers gather gray hairs.
Please see **JSON_REPLACE()** as a possible alternative.

JSON_REPLACE

JSON_REPLACE() is for updating existing values in a JSON
document. The path-value pair for an existing path in the
document overwrites the existing value in the document with the
new value. The path-value pair for a path that is nonexistent in
the document is ignored and has no effect. The server will
report an error if the json_doc argument is not a valid JSON
document, any path argument is not a valid path expression, or
it contains a * or ** wildcard. Note that: The path-value pairs
are evaluated from the left to the right.

Format: **JSON_REPLACE(json_doc, path, val[, path, val] ...)**

```
MySQL  localhost:33060+ ssl  testjson  SQL > UPDATE y SET x =
                           -> JSON_REPLACE(x,"$.key1","Value1A","$.key3","VALUE-
Query OK, 1 row affected (0.0159 sec)

Rows matched: 1  Changed: 1  Warnings: 0
 MySQL  localhost:33060+ ssl  testjson  SQL > SELECT * FROM y;
+-----------------------------------------------------+
| x                                                   |
+-----------------------------------------------------+
| {"key1": "Value1A", "key2": "value2", "key3": "VALUE-3"} |
+-----------------------------------------------------+
1 row in set (0.0008 sec)
 MySQL  localhost:33060+ ssl  testjson  SQL >
```

```
mysql> SELECT * FROM y;
+------------------------------------------------------+
| x                                                    |
+------------------------------------------------------+
| {"key1": "value1", "key2": "value2", "key3": "value3"} |
+------------------------------------------------------+
1 row in set (0.00 sec)

mysql> UPDATE y SET x =
JSON_REPLACE(x,"$.key1","Value1A","$.key3","VALUE-3");
Query OK, 1 row affected (0.01 sec)
Rows matched: 1  Changed: 1  Warnings: 0

mysql> SELECT * FROM y;
+-------------------------------------------------------+
| x                                                     |
+-------------------------------------------------------+
| {"key1": "Value 1A", "key2": "value2", "key3": "VALUE-3"} |
+-------------------------------------------------------+
1 row in set (0.00 sec)

mysql>
```

Example 5-11 -- Using JSON_REPLACE to update values

JSON_REMOVE

The counterpart to **JSON_SET()** is **JSON_REMOVE()** and is used to delete data from the JSON document. If the element to be removed does not exist in the document the server does not denote it as an error and it does not affect the document. The server will report an error if the json_doc argument is not a valid JSON document, any path argument is not a valid path expression, or it contains a * or ** wildcard. Note that: The path-value pairs are evaluated from the left to the right.

Format: **JSON_REMOVE(json_doc, path[, path] ...)**

```
MySQL  localhost:33060+ ssl  testjson  SQL > UPDATE y
                                         -> SET x = JSON_REMOVE(x,"$.key2"
Query OK, 1 row affected (0.0226 sec)

Rows matched: 1  Changed: 1  Warnings: 0
 MySQL  localhost:33060+ ssl  testjson  SQL > SELECT * FROM y;
+------------------------------------+
| x                                  |
+------------------------------------+
| {"key1": "Value1A", "key3": "VALUE-3"} |
+------------------------------------+
1 row in set (0.0009 sec)
 MySQL  localhost:33060+ ssl  testjson  SQL >
```

```
mysql> SELECT * FROM y;

+-----------------------------------------------------------+
| x                                                         |
+-----------------------------------------------------------+
| {"key1": "Value 1A", "key2": "value2", "key3": "VALUE-3"} |
+-----------------------------------------------------------+
1 row in set (0.00 sec)

mysql> UPDATE y
       SET x = JSON_REMOVE(x,"$.key2");
Query OK, 1 row affected (0.00 sec)
Rows matched: 1  Changed: 1  Warnings: 0

mysql> SELECT * FROM y;
```

```
+-----------------------------------------+
| x                                       |
+-----------------------------------------+
| {"key1": "Value 1A", "key3": "VALUE-3"} |
+-----------------------------------------+
`1 row in set (0.00 sec)


mysql>
```

Example 5-12 -- Using JSON_REMOVE to change a document

So **JSON_REMOVE()** will remove one or more key/values. In
cases where all the key/values need to be removed it may be
easier to use **JSON_SET()** and set the document to a blank or NULL
rather than specify each key for the given document.

JSON_SET

The **JSON_SET()** function Inserts or updates data in a JSON
document and returns the result. If the path-value pair for an
existing path is found in the document, the new value will
overwrite the old value. But if the path-value pair is
nonexistent in the path of the document it will be added to the
document or the member is added to the object and associated
with the new value. If a position value is past the end of an
existing array it will be extended with the new value. The
server will report an error if the json_doc argument is not a
valid JSON document, any path argument is not a valid path

67

expression, or it contains a * or ** wildcard. Note that: The path-value pairs are evaluated from the left to the right.

Format: **JSON_SET(json_doc, path, val[, path, val] ...)**

```
MySQL  localhost:33060+ ssl  testjson  SQL > UPDATE y
                                         -> SET x =
                                         -> JSON_SET(x,"$.key1","Value 1X","$.key99","Value-99");
Query OK, 1 row affected (0.0149 sec)

Rows matched: 1  Changed: 1  Warnings: 0
MySQL  localhost:33060+ ssl  testjson  SQL > SELECT * FROM y;
+--------------------------------------------------------+
| x                                                      |
+--------------------------------------------------------+
| {"key1": "Value 1X", "key3": "VALUE-3", "key99": "Value-99"} |
+--------------------------------------------------------+
1 row in set (0.0009 sec)
MySQL  localhost:33060+ ssl  testjson  SQL >
```

```
mysql> SELECT * FROM y;

    +---------------------------------------+
    | x                                     |
    +---------------------------------------+
    | {"key1": "Value 1A", "key3": "VALUE-3"} |
    +---------------------------------------+
    1 row in set (0.00 sec)

mysql> UPDATE y
    SET x =
    JSON_SET(x,"$.key1","Value 1X","$.key99","Value-99");
    Query OK, 1 row affected (0.00 sec)
    Rows matched: 1  Changed: 1  Warnings: 0

mysql> SELECT * FROM y;
    +---------------------------------------------------------+
    | x                                                       |
    +---------------------------------------------------------+
```

```
| {"key1": "Value 1X", "key3": "VALUE-3", "key99": "Value-99"} |
+-------------------------------------------------------------+
1 row in set (0.00 sec)


mysql>
```

Example 5-13 -- Using JSON_SET to replace the value of $.key1 and to add a new value for $.key99

JSON_SET will set values for an already defined key (the value of "key1" was changed from "Value 1A" to "Value 1X". And nonexistent keyS/values are inserted as directed.

JSON_UNQUOTE

The JSON standards describe how keys and values can be quoted to improve their integrity as they are transferred about. Unfortunately this protection may not be needed by the downstream function or application and needs to be stripped. The function or application can be engineered to do this but it is often much simpler to have the database do this work. And it can be aliased with the ->> operator.

Format: **JSON_UNQUOTE(json_val)**

```
MySQL  localhost:33060+ ssl  testjson  SQL > SELECT JSON_EXTRACT(x,"$.key1") FROM y;
+-------------------------+
| JSON_EXTRACT(x,"$.key1") |
+-------------------------+
| "Value 1X"              |
+-------------------------+
1 row in set (0.0005 sec)
MySQL  localhost:33060+ ssl  testjson  SQL > SELECT JSON_UNQUOTE(JSON_EXTRACT(x,"$.key1"))
                                         ->    FROM y;
+---------------------------------------+
| JSON_UNQUOTE(JSON_EXTRACT(x,"$.key1")) |
+---------------------------------------+
| Value 1X                              |
+---------------------------------------+
1 row in set (0.0003 sec)
MySQL  localhost:33060+ ssl  testjson  SQL >
MySQL  localhost:33060+ ssl  testjson  SQL > SELECT x->>"$.key1"
                                         ->    FROM y;
+-------------+
| x->>"$.key1" |
+-------------+
| Value 1X    |
+-------------+
1 row in set (0.0004 sec)
MySQL  localhost:33060+ ssl  testjson  SQL >
```

```
mysql> SELECT * FROM y;

+-------------------------------------------------------------+
| x                                                           |
+-------------------------------------------------------------+
| {"key1": "Value 1X", "key3": "VALUE-3", "key99": "Value-99"} |
+-------------------------------------------------------------+
1 row in set (0.00 sec)


mysql> SELECT JSON_EXTRACT(x,"$.key1") FROM y;

+-------------------------+
| JSON_EXTRACT(x,"$.key1") |
+-------------------------+
| "Value 1X"              |
+-------------------------+
1 row in set (0.00 sec)


mysql> SELECT JSON_UNQUOTE(JSON_EXTRACT(x,"$.key1"))
```

```
        FROM y;
+---------------------------------------+
| JSON_UNQUOTE(JSON_EXTRACT(x,"$.key1")) |
+---------------------------------------+
| Value 1X                              |
+---------------------------------------+
1 row in set (0.00 sec)


mysql> SELECT x->>"$.key1"
        FROM y;
+-------------+
| x->>"$.key1" |
+-------------+
| Value 1X    |
+-------------+
1 row in set (0.00 sec)


mysql>
```

Example 5-14 -- Using JSON_UNQUOTE() and the ->>
operator to strip quotes. The choice to use the ->>
operator over JSON_UNQUOTE() with JSON_EXTRACT() is a
matter of choice, read-ability, and style. But older
versions of MySQL will not have the ->> operator (MySQL
5.7.13 was its introduction.

The Three JSON_MERGE Functions

Warning! There are *three* JSON Merge Functions --
JSON_MERGE(), **JSON_MERGE_PRESERVE()**, and **JSON_MERGE_PATH()** are

very easy to mistake for one another but have much different effects on the data. To add to any possible confusion it needs to be made clear that **JSON_MERGE()** is a synonym for **JSON_MERGE_PRESERVE()** which means there were really two functions with three names. **JSON_MERGE()** was deprecated in MySQL version 8.0.3 and will likely be removed in future releases.

So why three separate MERGE functions? The original **JSON_MERGE()** did not act like other similar functions in programming languages like Python. Feedback from early users was mixed, with some loving the original while others wanted it to match JSON merge functions in their favorite language. So what does the 'standard' say as it has to be the definitive statement on the subject. Well, not so much in this case. RFC7159 states that object names should be unique. The implications of this are that duplicates are not supposed to happen and the implementation is left up to the developer. So **JSON_MERGE_PATH()** was created to pair with the original function, now renamed to **MYSQL_JSON_PRESERVE()**.

So what are the differences between **JSON_MERGE()**/**JSON_MERGE_PRESERVE()** and **JSON_MERGE_PATH()**? The former merges two or more JSON documents and returns the merged result. The latter merges two or more JSON documents, returning the merged result, without preserving members having duplicate keys and drops any member in the first object whose key is matched in the second object.

The following example clearly shows the **JSON_MERGE()**/**JSON_MERGE_PRESERVE()** cleaning merging the two JSON objects while preserving all the values but **JSON_MERGE_PATH()**

keeping only the latest versions of the key/values after the
merge.

```
MySQL  localhost:33060+ ssl  testjson  SQL > SELECT
                         -> JSON_MERGE('{ "odds" : 1, "evens" : 2 }',
                         -> '{ "odds": 3, "evens" : 4 }');
+-----------------------------------------------------------+
| JSON_MERGE('{ "odds" : 1, "evens" : 2 }',
'{ "odds": 3, "evens" : 4 }') |
+-----------------------------------------------------------+
| {"odds": [1, 3], "evens": [2, 4]}                         |
+-----------------------------------------------------------+
1 row in set, 1 warning (0.0006 sec)
Warning (code 1287): 'JSON_MERGE' is deprecated and will be removed in a future release. Please use JSON_MERGE_PRESERVE/JSON_MER
GE_PATCH instead
MySQL  localhost:33060+ ssl  testjson  SQL > SELECT
                         -> JSON_MERGE_PRESERVE('{ "odds" : 1, "evens" : 2 }',
                         -> '{ "odds": 3, "evens" : 4 }');
+-----------------------------------------------------------+
| JSON_MERGE_PRESERVE('{ "odds" : 1, "evens" : 2 }',
'{ "odds": 3, "evens" : 4 }') |
+-----------------------------------------------------------+
| {"odds": [1, 3], "evens": [2, 4]}                         |
+-----------------------------------------------------------+
1 row in set (0.0004 sec)
MySQL  localhost:33060+ ssl  testjson  SQL > select
                         -> JSON_MERGE_PATCH('{ "odds" : 1, "evens" : 2 }',
                         -> '{ "odds": 3, "evens" : 4 }');
+-----------------------------------------------------------+
| JSON_MERGE_PATCH('{ "odds" : 1, "evens" : 2 }',
'{ "odds": 3, "evens" : 4 }') |
+-----------------------------------------------------------+
| {"odds": 3, "evens": 4}                                   |
+-----------------------------------------------------------+
1 row in set (0.0003 sec)
MySQL  localhost:33060+ ssl  testjson  SQL >
```

```
mysql> SELECT
        JSON_MERGE('{ "odds" : 1, "evens" : 2 }',
        '{ "odds": 3, "evens" : 4 }');
+-----------------------------------------------------------------------+
| JSON_MERGE('{ "odds" : 1, "evens" : 2 }','{ "odds": 3, "evens" : 4 }') |
+-----------------------------------------------------------------------+
| {"odds": [1, 3], "evens": [2, 4]}                                     |
+-----------------------------------------------------------------------+
1 row in set, 1 warning (0.00 sec)


mysql> SELECT
        JSON_MERGE_PRESERVE('{ "odds" : 1, "evens" : 2 }',
        '{ "odds": 3, "evens" : 4 }');
+-----------------------------------------------------------------------+
| JSON_MERGE_PRESERVE('{ "odds" : 1, "evens" : 2 }','{ "odds": 3, "evens" : 4 }') |
+-----------------------------------------------------------------------+
| {"odds": [1, 3], "evens": [2, 4]}                                     |
+-----------------------------------------------------------------------+
1 row in set (0.00 sec)
```

```
mysql> select
       JSON_MERGE_PATCH('{ "odds" : 1, "evens" : 2 }',
       '{ "odds": 3, "evens" : 4 }');
+----------------------------------------------------------------------+
| JSON_MERGE_PATCH('{ "odds" : 1, "evens" : 2 }','{ "odds": 3, "evens" : 4 }') |
+----------------------------------------------------------------------+
| {"odds": 3, "evens": 4}                                              |
+----------------------------------------------------------------------+
1 row in set (0.00 sec)
```

Example 5-15 -- How the various JSON_MERGE functions operate. Be sure to check your version of MySQL to ensure your query works as desired.

JSON_MERGE

Format: **JSON_MERGE(json_doc, json_doc[, json_doc] ...)**

The **JSON_MERGE()** function has had a lot of changes since the first version came to light. The original intent was fairly simple as can be seen in the example below:

```
mysql> select JSON_MERGE('{ "odds" : 1, "evens" : 2 }','{ "odds": 3, "evens" : 4 }');
+----------------------------------------------------------------------+
| JSON_MERGE('{ "odds" : 1, "evens" : 2 }','{ "odds": 3, "evens" : 4 }') |
+----------------------------------------------------------------------+
```

```
| {"odds": [1, 3], "evens": [2, 4]}                                       |
+-------------------------------------------------------------------------+
1 row in set (0.00 sec)


mysql>
```


Example 5-16 -- Merging two JSON documents (MySQL 5.7)

The two documents had their adjacent keys matched and then
their values merged. Depending on data type, array or object,
were combined into one array or object. A scalar auto wrapped as
an array and merged as an array. And an adjacent array and
object are merged by auto wrapping the object as an array and
merging them as two arrays.

```
mysql> SELECT * from y;
+----------------------------------------------------------------+
| x                                                              |
+----------------------------------------------------------------+
| {"key1": "Value 1X", "key3": "VALUE-3", "key99": "Value-99"}   |
+----------------------------------------------------------------+
1 row in set (0.00 sec)


mysql> SELECT JSON_MERGE(x->"$",'{ "key2" : "Buzz" }')
       FROM y;

+-------------------------------------------------------------------------+
```

```
| JSON_MERGE(x->"$",'{ "key2" : "Buzz" }')                                         |
+----------------------------------------------------------------------------------+
| {"key1": "Value 1X", "key2": "Buzz", "key3": "VALUE-3", "key99": "Value-99"} |
+----------------------------------------------------------------------------------+
1 row in set (0.00 sec)

mysql>
```

Example 5-17 -- Using JSON_MERGE to combine data

Notice that the keys are sorted!

But there was an issue with the Last Version Wins
precedence. Last Version Wins is common in most scripting
languages such as PHP's json_merge function. And this approach
would be more consistent with other MySQL JSON functions. So
JSON_MERGE will change with the release of MySQL. Example 5-12
above shows two arrays in the SQL statement, **SELECT
JSON_MERGE('{ "odds" : 1, "evens" : 2 }','{ "odds": 3, "evens" :
4 }');** and with Last Version Wins the output will be:

```
mysql> SELECT JSON_MERGE('{ "odds" : 1, "evens" : 2 }',
       '{ "odds": 3, "evens" : 4 }');
+----------------------------------------------------------------------+
| JSON_MERGE('{ "odds" : 1, "evens" : 2 }','{ "odds": 3, "evens" : 4 }') |
+----------------------------------------------------------------------+
| {"odds": [3], "evens": [ 4]}                                          |
+----------------------------------------------------------------------+
1 row in set (0.00 sec)
```

Example 5-18 -- JSON_MERGE and Last Version Wins Precedence (MySQL 8.0.3 onwards) with Last Version Wins

JSON_MERGE_PRESERVE

Format : **JSON_MERGE_PRESERVE(json_doc, json_doc[, json_doc] ...)**

The **JSON_MERGE_PRESERVE()** function was created to provide the functionality of the original **JSON_MERGE()** where Last Version Wins was not considered. Read the section above for the MySQL 5.7 version of **JSON_MERGE()** for an example of how this function performs.

JSON_DEPTH

JSON_DEPTH() reports the JSON document's maximum depth, or a NULL if there is no document. Empty arrays, objects, scalars will have a depth of 1. An array containing only elements of depth 1 or non-empty objects containing only member values of depth 1 has depth 2. The depth level is increased by one by non-empty json arrays or by non-empty json objects.

Format: **JSON_DEPTH(json_doc)**

```
MySQL  localhost:33060+ ssl  testjson  SQL > use world_x;
Default schema set to `world_x`.
Fetching table and column names from `world_x` for auto-completion... Press ^C to stop.
MySQL  localhost:33060+ ssl  world_x  SQL > SELECT JSON_DEPTH(doc),JSON_KEYS(doc) FROM countryinfo WHERE _id = 'USA';
+-----------------+-----------------------------------------------------------------------+
| JSON_DEPTH(doc) | JSON_KEYS(doc)                                                        |
+-----------------+-----------------------------------------------------------------------+
|               3 | ["GNP", "_id", "Name", "IndepYear", "geography", "government", "demographics"] |
+-----------------+-----------------------------------------------------------------------+
1 row in set (0.0010 sec)
MySQL  localhost:33060+ ssl  world_x  SQL >
```

```
mysql> SELECT JSON_DEPTH(doc),JSON_KEYS(doc) FROM
countryinfo WHERE _id = 'USA';

+-----------------+-----------------------------------------------------------------------+
| JSON_DEPTH(doc) | JSON_KEYS(doc)                                                        |
+-----------------+-----------------------------------------------------------------------+
|               3 | ["GNP", "_id", "Name", "IndepYear", "geography", "government", "demographics"] |
+-----------------+-----------------------------------------------------------------------+
1 row in set (0.00 sec)
```

Example 5-19 -- Example of JSON_DEPTH

JSON_LENGTH

JSON_LENGTH() reports the length of a JSON document or the length of path of one if provided.   It is easy to see where the information comes from when used with the JSON_KEYS function.

Format: **JSON_LENGTH(json_doc[, path])**

```
MySQL  localhost:33060+ ssl  world_x  SQL > SELECT JSON_KEYS(doc),
                                    -> JSON_LENGTH(doc)
                                    -> FROM countryinfo
                                    -> LIMIT 1;
+-----------------------------------------------------------------------+-----------------+
| JSON_KEYS(doc)                                                        | JSON_LENGTH(doc) |
+-----------------------------------------------------------------------+-----------------+
| ["GNP", "_id", "Name", "IndepYear", "geography", "government", "demographics"] |               7 |
+-----------------------------------------------------------------------+-----------------+
1 row in set (0.0007 sec)
MySQL  localhost:33060+ ssl  world_x  SQL >
```

78

```
mysql> SELECT JSON_KEYS(doc),
       JSON_LENGTH(doc)
       FROM countryinfo
       LIMIT 1;          +------------------------------------------------------------
---------------+-----------------+
| JSON_KEYS(doc)                                                              | LSON_LENGTH(doc) |
+----------------------------------------------------------------------------+-----------------+
| ["GNP", "_id", "Name", "IndepYear", "geography", "government", "demographics"] |               7 |
+----------------------------------------------------------------------------+-----------------+
1 row in set (0.00 sec)
```

Example 5-20 -- Using JSON_LENGTH

The length of a document is as follows: Scalars have a
length of one. Array length is the number of items in the array
and objects are the number of objects in the array. Nested
arrays or objects are not counted. In Example 16-16 it is easy
to see from the output of **JSON_KEYS** the corresponding length of
the JSON document.

```
MySQL  localhost:33060+ ssl  world_x  SQL > SELECT JSON_KEYS(doc,'$.geography'),
                                     ->            JSON_LENGTH(doc,'$.geography')
                                     ->            FROM countryinfo LIMIT 1;
+-------------------------------------+-------------------------------+
| JSON_KEYS(doc,'$.geography')        | JSON_LENGTH(doc,'$.geography') |
+-------------------------------------+-------------------------------+
| ["Region", "Continent", "SurfaceArea"] |                            3 |
+-------------------------------------+-------------------------------+
1 row in set (0.0005 sec)
MySQL  localhost:33060+ ssl  world_x  SQL >
```

```
mysql> SELECT JSON_KEYS(doc,'$.geography'),
          JSON_LENGTH(doc,'$.geography')
          FROM countryinfo LIMIT 1;
+-------------------------------------+-------------------------------+
| json_keys(doc,'$.geography')        | json_length(doc,'$.geography') |
+-------------------------------------+-------------------------------+
```

```
| ["Region", "Continent", "SurfaceArea"] |                                    3 |
+---------------------------------------+--------------------------------+
1 row in set (0.00 sec)
```

Example 5-21 -- Using JSON_LENGTH to investigate a second level document path

JSON_TYPE

The **JSON_TYPE()** function returns a UTF8MB4 string reporting on the contents of a JSON value -- array, object, integer, double, and null.

Format: **JSON_TYPE(json_val)**

```
MySQL  localhost:33060+ ssl  world_x  SQL > SELECT JSON_TYPE('[1,2,3]'),
                                         -> JSON_TYPE('{ "x":"y"}'),
                                         -> JSON_TYPE('123'),
                                         -> JSON_TYPE(NULL)\G
*************************** 1. row ***************************
    JSON_TYPE('[1,2,3]'): ARRAY
JSON_TYPE('{ "x":"y"}'): OBJECT
       JSON_TYPE('123'): INTEGER
      JSON_TYPE(NULL): NULL
1 row in set (0.0007 sec)
MySQL  localhost:33060+ ssl  world_x  SQL >
```

```
mysql> SELECT JSON_TYPE('[1,2,3]'),
                    JSON_TYPE('{ "x":"y"}'),
                    JSON_TYPE('123'),
                    JSON_TYPE(NULL)\G
```

```
*************************** 1. row
***************************
        JSON_TYPE('[1,2,3]'): ARRAY
JSON_TYPE('{ "x" : "y" }'): OBJECT
          JSON_TYPE('123'): INTEGER
          JSON_TYPE(NULL): NULL
1 row in set (0.00 sec)

mysql>
```

Example 5-22 -- Using JSON_TYPE to determine the data type

JSON_VALID

The use of **JSON_VALID()** on a JSON document to test for validity before attempted insertion into the database could save a great deal of time. The MySQL Server will reject invalid JSON documents and **JSON_VALID()** can be used to double check document validity before insertion into the database.

Format: **JSON_VALID(val)**

```
MySQL  localhost:33060+ ssl  world_x  SQL > SELECT JSON_VALID('{ "A" : 1}'),
                                     ->            JSON_VALID('A'),
                                     ->            JSON_VALID('"A"')\G
*************************** 1. row ***************************
JSON_VALID('{ "A" : 1}'): 1
      JSON_VALID('A'): 0
    JSON_VALID('"A"'): 1
1 row in set (0.0003 sec)
MySQL  localhost:33060+ ssl  world_x  SQL >
```

```
mysql> SELECT JSON_VALID('{ "A" : 1}'),
            JSON_VALID('A'),
            JSON_VALID('"A"')\G
*************************** 1. row
***************************
JSON_VALID('{ "A" : 1}'): 1
         JSON_VALID('A'): 0
       JSON_VALID('"A"'): 1
1 row in set (0.00 sec)

mysql>
```

Example 5-23 -- Using JSON_VALID() to ensure validity of JSON documents. Note this first tested object is a valid JSON object and the third is itself a valid JSON document. But the second test fails as it is invalid JSON.

Remember that the MySQL server will reject invalid JSON documents. In Example 5-23 all the expressions are not valid JSON so the server returns a zero.

JSON_STORAGE_SIZE

The **JSON_STORAGE_SIZE()** function reports the size in bytes needed to store the binary representation of the JSON document when it was inserted.

Format: **JSON_STORAGE_SIZE(json_val)**

```
MySQL  localhost:33060+ ssl  world_x  SQL > SELECT JSON_EXTRACT(doc,'$.Name'),
                                    ->            JSON_STORAGE_SIZE(doc)
                                    ->       FROM countryinfo
                                    ->       WHERE _id IN ("USA","BRA")
                                    -> ;
+---------------------------+------------------------+
| JSON_EXTRACT(doc,'$.Name') | JSON_STORAGE_SIZE(doc) |
+---------------------------+------------------------+
| "Brazil"                  |                    342 |
| "United States"           |                    338 |
+---------------------------+------------------------+
2 rows in set (0.0014 sec)
MySQL  localhost:33060+ ssl  world_x  SQL >
```

```
mysql> SELECT JSON_EXTRACT(doc,'$.Name'),
              JSON_STORAGE_SIZE(doc)
         FROM countryinfo
         WHERE _id IN ("USA","BRA");
+---------------------------+------------------------+
| JSON_EXTRACT(doc,'$.Name') | JSON_STORAGE_SIZE(doc) |
+---------------------------+------------------------+
| "Brazil"                  |                    342 |
| "United States"           |                    338 |
+---------------------------+------------------------+
2 rows in set (0.01 sec)
```

Example 5-24 -- Determining document storage size with JSON_STORAGE_SIZE. The size of a document on disk is roughly one gigabyte but it can be larger while being manipulated in memory.

JSON_STORAGE_FREE

The **JSON_FREE_FUNCTION()** reports the amount storage space
was freed in bytes in its binary representation after it was
updated. The updates need to be in place (not rewriting the
entire document) using **JSON_SET()**, **JSON_REMOVE()**, or
JSON_REPLACE(). It will return a zero if the argument is a JSON
document in a string.

Format: **JSON_STORAGE_FREE(json_val)**


```
mysql> CREATE DATABASE  IF NOT EXISTS test; USE test;
mysql> CREATE TABLE x (id INT UNSIGNED, doc JSON);
mysql> INSERT INTO x VALUES (1,'{"a" : "1"}');
mysql> UPDATE x
       SET doc =
       JSON_SET(doc,'$[0]','{ "a" : "This is a string" }');
Query OK, 1 row affected (0.01 sec)
Rows matched: 1  Changed: 1  Warnings: 0


mysql> UPDATE x
       SET doc = JSON_SET(doc,'$.a','{ "a" : "a" }');
Query OK, 1 row affected (0.01 sec)
Rows matched: 1  Changed: 1  Warnings: 0


mysql> SELECT JSON_STORAGE_FREE(doc) FROM x;
+-----------------------+
| JSON_STORAGE_FREE(doc) |
+-----------------------+
|                    15 |
+-----------------------+
```

```
1 row in set (0.00 sec)
```

Example 5-25 -- Example of using JSON_STORAGE_FREE()
by changing 'This is a string', which is 16 characters, to
'a', which is one character or a net change of 15 bytes.

Chapter 6

JSON and Non JSON OUTPUT

The advantages of traditional relational data and schema less data are both large. But there may be cases where what is in a schema needs to be schema less or what is schema less needs to be in a schema. Both approaches are easy to do.

JSON Formatted Data

The various JSON functions supplied by MySQL can also be used to create JSON formatted output from non JSON data. The first example is of non JSON data output in a non JSON format as has been the standard for MySQL for much of its existence. .

```
MySQL  localhost:33060+ ssl  world_x  SQL > SELECT city.Name,
                                        ->        country.Name
                                        -> FROM city
                                        -> JOIN country ON (city.CountryCode=country.Code)
                                        -> LIMIT 5;
+----------------+-------------+
| Name           | Name        |
+----------------+-------------+
| Kabul          | Afghanistan |
| Qandahar       | Afghanistan |
| Herat          | Afghanistan |
| Mazar-e-Sharif | Afghanistan |
| Amsterdam      | Netherlands |
+----------------+-------------+
5 rows in set (0.0015 sec)
MySQL  localhost:33060+ ssl  world_x  SQL >
```

```
mysql> SELECT city.Name,
              country.Name
         FROM city
         JOIN country ON
(city.CountryCode=country.Code)
         LIMIT 5;
+----------------+-------------+
| Name           | Name        |
+----------------+-------------+
| Kabul          | Afghanistan |
| Qandahar       | Afghanistan |
| Herat          | Afghanistan |
| Mazar-e-Sharif | Afghanistan |
| Amsterdam      | Netherlands |
+----------------+-------------+
5 rows in set (0.00 sec)
```

Example 6-1 -- Non JSON data and output from a relational table

This is a fairly typical example of MySQL output for a fairly regular query. This good old MySQL at its finest. But not very useful if that data is needed by something that consumes data in a JSON format.

JSON_OBJECT

The query from Example 6-1 can quickly be adapted to output non JSON data in a JSON format. JSON objects can easily be created with **JSON_OBJECT()** but remember that in JSON objects are pairs (key/value pairs) so no odd number of arguments.

Format: **JSON_OBJECT([key, val[, key, val] ...])**

Below strings are added to the previous query to create keys for the values. Neither "City" nor "Country" are table row names; both are named 'Name' which can be confusing for casual readers and the server.

```
mysql> SELECT
    JSON_OBJECT("City", city.Name, "Country", country.Name)
    FROM city
    JOIN country ON (city.CountryCode=country.Code)
            LIMIT 5;
+----------------------------------------------------------+
| JSON_OBJECT("City", city.Name, "Country", country.Name)  |
+----------------------------------------------------------+
| {"City": "Kabul", "Country": "Afghanistan"}              |
| {"City": "Qandahar", "Country": "Afghanistan"}           |
```

```
| {"City": "Herat", "Country": "Afghanistan"}          |
| {"City": "Mazar-e-Sharif", "Country": "Afghanistan"} |
| {"City": "Amsterdam", "Country": "Netherlands"}      |
+------------------------------------------------------+
5 rows in set (0.00 sec)
```

Example 6-2 -- Using JSON_OBJECT() with non-JSON data

So the non JSON data is now in a JSON format. You can use both non-JSON and JSON columns as arguments to this function.

JSON_ARRAY

In a similar fashion to using **JSON_OBJECT()**, **JSON_ARRAY()** can be used to create arrays from non-JSON data.

Format: **JSON_ARRAY([val[, val] ...])**

```
MySQL  localhost:33060+ ssl  world_x  SQL > SELECT JSON_ARRAY(Code, Name, Capital)
                                      ->     FROM country
                                      ->     LIMIT 1;
+------------------------------+
| JSON_ARRAY(Code, Name, Capital) |
+------------------------------+
| ["ABW", "Aruba", 129]        |
+------------------------------+
1 row in set (0.0005 sec)
MySQL  localhost:33060+ ssl  world_x  SQL >
```

```
mysql> SELECT JSON_ARRAY(Code, Name, Capital)
       FROM country
       LIMIT 1;
+--------------------------------+
```

```
| json_array(Code, Name, Capital) |
+---------------------------------+
| ["ABW", "Aruba", 129]           |
+---------------------------------+
1 row in set (0.00 sec)
```

Example 6-3 Using JSON_ARRAY with non-JSON data

Examples 6-2 and 6-3 show how traditional MySQL data can now be formatted as JSON objects or arrays. And of course you can mix and match JSON and non JSON columns into arrays or objects.

Casting

MySQL allows casting of one data type as another. This includes JSON. And casting from within MySQL was around for decades before the JSON Data Type.

```
MySQL  localhost:33060+ ssl  world_x  SQL > SELECT JSON_TYPE(CAST('[1,2]' AS JSON
+---------------------------------+
| JSON_TYPE(CAST('[1,2]' AS JSON)) |
+---------------------------------+
| ARRAY                           |
+---------------------------------+
1 row in set (0.0004 sec)
MySQL  localhost:33060+ ssl  world_x  SQL > SELECT JSON_TYPE(CAST('1' AS JSON));
+---------------------------+
| JSON_TYPE(CAST('1' AS JSON)) |
+---------------------------+
| INTEGER                   |
+---------------------------+
1 row in set (0.0003 sec)
MySQL  localhost:33060+ ssl  world_x  SQL >
```

```
mysql> SELECT JSON_TYPE(CAST('[1,2]' AS JSON));
+---------------------------------+
| JSON_TYPE(CAST('[1,2]' AS JSON)) |
+---------------------------------+
| ARRAY                           |
+---------------------------------+
1 row in set (0.00 sec)


mysql> SELECT JSON_TYPE(CAST('1' AS JSON));
+-----------------------------+
| JSON_TYPE(CAST('1' AS JSON)) |
+-----------------------------+
| INTEGER                     |
+-----------------------------+
1 row in set (0.00 sec)


mysql>
```

Example 6-4 -- Casting data as JSON

Be sure to read the information on **JSON_VALUE()** for times when you need to cast values from a JSON document to a certain type.

Conversely JSON data can be cast as other data types.

```
MySQL  localhost:33060+ ssl  world_x  SQL > SELECT CAST(JSON_EXTRACT(doc,"$.demographics.LifeExpectancy") AS unsigned)
                              -> FROM countryinfo WHERE _id = 'USA';
+----------------------------------------------------------------------+
| CAST(JSON_EXTRACT(doc,"$.demographics.LifeExpectancy") AS unsigned) |
+----------------------------------------------------------------------+
|                                                                 77 |
+----------------------------------------------------------------------+
1 row in set (0.0006 sec)
MySQL  localhost:33060+ ssl  world_x  SQL >
```

```
mysql> SELECT
CAST(JSON_EXTRACT(doc,"$.demographics.LifeExpectancy") AS
unsigned)
        FROM countryinfo
        WHERE _id = 'USA';
+----------------------------------------------------------------------+
| CAST(JSON_EXTRACT(doc,"$.demographics.LifeExpectancy") AS unsigned) |
+----------------------------------------------------------------------+
|                                                                 77 |
+----------------------------------------------------------------------+
1 row in set (0.00 sec)
```

Example 6-5 -- Casting a JSON DOUBLE into an INTEGER

Be careful to fully provide the path of the JSON key you
are searching or the server will return NULL. Wildcards will
also cause problems as can been see in the next example.

```
mysql> SELECT
json_extract(doc,"$.demographics.LifeExpectancy")
        FROM countryinfo
        WHERE _id = 'USA';
+----------------------------------------------------+
```

```
| json_extract(doc,"$.demographics.LifeExpectancy") |
+---------------------------------------------------+
| 77.0999984741211                                  |
+---------------------------------------------------+
1 row in set (0.00 sec)
```

```
mysql> SELECT
CAST(json_extract(doc,"$.demographics.LifeExpectancy") AS
UNSIGNED)
FROM countryinfo
WHERE _id = 'USA';
+------------------------------------------------------------------+
| CAST(json_extract(doc,"$.demographics.LifeExpectancy") AS UNSIGNED) |
+------------------------------------------------------------------+
|                                                               77 |
+------------------------------------------------------------------+
```

Example 6-7 -- How casting as an INTEGER changes effects the data

Example 6-7 shows how calling the same information will a wildcard in the path in **JSON_EXTRACT()** will return an array while without the data is a double. When in doubt, cast your values to what you need. This is especially important when matching data values with indexes as it provides the query optimizer with valuable information for building query plans.

For information on casting data within a JSON document to another value please see the section on **JSON_VALUE()** in Chapter 4.

Non JSON Output

Transforming JSON data into *temporary* relational tables is done with the **JSON_TABLE** which first appeared in MySQL 8. Once the NoSQL JSON data is 'cast' into a relational table, that relational table can be processed with the very powerful SQL functions available in MySQL.

Format **JSON_TABLE(doc,path, columns (name type PATH path),...) AS**

Temptable-name

The power to map JSON data into temporary relational tables and then query from those tables opens up the power of relational data processing without having to establish generated columns, hard to debug stored procedures, or creating views.

```
MySQL  localhost:33060+ ssl  world_x  SQL > SELECT country_name,
   ->                    IndyYear
   -> FROM countryinfo,
   -> JSON_TABLE(doc, "$" COLUMNS (
   ->   country_name CHAR(20) PATH "$.Name",
   ->   IndyYear INT PATH "$.IndepYear")) as st
   -> WHERE IndyYear > 1992;
+----------------+----------+
| country_name   | IndyYear |
+----------------+----------+
| Czech Republic |     1993 |
| Eritrea        |     1993 |
| Palau          |     1994 |
| Slovakia       |     1993 |
+----------------+----------+
4 rows in set (0.0009 sec)
MySQL  localhost:33060+ ssl  world_x  SQL >
```

```
mysql> SELECT country_name,
               IndyYear
       FROM countryinfo,
       JSON_TABLE(doc, "$" COLUMNS (
```

```
      country_name CHAR(20) PATH "$.Name",
      IndyYear INT PATH "$.IndepYear")) as stuff
    WHERE IndyYear > 1992;
+----------------+----------+
| country_name   | IndyYear |
+----------------+----------+
| Czech Republic |     1993 |
| Eritrea        |     1993 |
| Palau          |     1994 |
| Slovakia       |     1993 |
+----------------+----------+
4 rows in set, 67 warnings (0.08 sec)

mysql>
```

Example 6-9 - Using JSON_TABLE() to convert JSON data into a relational table. Once we have the relational table it is easy to use like any other relational table and winnow down results with the WHERE clause.

In Example 6-7 two JSON key/value pairs are extracted, formatted, and then returned in a table. Note that the two columns, country_name and IndyYear, are only named within the **JSON_TABLE()**. The first argument to the function is the JSON column in the table to be used and then the path is specified. The $ path can be used to specify the entire document or a sub-path can be specified.

This query also generated 67 warnings! Twenty of those can be easily removed by upping the CHAR(20) field for *country_name* to something longer like a CHAR(50). Truncating data can be dangerous and it would take some work to check all the documents to find the longest *Name* and then adjust the query to match. The other 47 warnings are invalid casting of a NULL to an integer. For this particular query the desired result was for countries with years of independence since 1993 it does not matter. But it would matter the desired result was, for illustration, independence years before 1515.

Missing Data

An interesting feature of **JSON_TABLE()** is the ability to specify what to do when the data is missing. Unlike a relational column where missing or NULL values can be stored, the JSON document has no guarantee that all desired key/value pairs exist.


```
mysql> SELECT * FROM t1;
+-----+------------------------+
| _id | doc                    |
+-----+------------------------+
|   1 | {"x": 0, "name": "Bill"} |
|   2 | {"x": 1, "name": "Mary"} |
|   3 | {"name": "Pete"}       |
+-----+------------------------+
3 rows in set (0.00 sec)

mysql>
```


Example 6-10 -- Sample data for JSON_TABLE

Example 6-8 -- Has a small dataset where all the columns have a 'name' key/value pair and the third record is missing a 'x' key/value pair. The DEFAULT ON EMPTY qualifier will be used to provide data for the missing 'x' key/value pair.

```
MySQL  localhost:33060+ ssl  test  SQL > SELECT * FROM t1,
                                 ->        JSON_TABLE(doc,"$" COLUMNS (
                                 ->        xHasValue INT PATH "$.x" DEFAULT '999' ON EMPTY,
                                 ->        hasname CHAR(10) EXISTS PATH "$.name",
                                 ->        mojo CHAR(5) EXISTS PATH "$.mojo"))
                                 ->        AS t2;
+------+------------------------+-----------+----------+------+
| _id | doc                     | xHasValue | hasname | mojo |
+------+------------------------+-----------+----------+------+
|   1 | {"x": "0", "name": "Bill"} |       0 | 1       | 0    |
|   1 | {"x": "1", "name": "Mary"} |       1 | 1       | 0    |
|   1 | {"name": "Pete"}           |     999 | 1       | 0    |
+------+------------------------+-----------+----------+------+
3 rows in set (0.0005 sec)
MySQL  localhost:33060+ ssl  test  SQL >
```

```
mysql> SELECT * FROM t1,
       JSON_TABLE(doc,"$" COLUMNS (
       xHasValue INT PATH "$.x" DEFAULT '999' ON EMPTY,
       hasname CHAR(10) EXISTS PATH "$.name",
       mojo CHAR(5) EXISTS PATH "$.mojo"))
       AS t2;
+-----+-------------------------+-----------+---------+------+
| _id | doc                     | xHasValue | hasname | mojo |
+-----+-------------------------+-----------+---------+------+
|   1 | {"x": 0, "name": "Bill"} |        0 | 1       |    0 |
|   2 | {"x": 1, "name": "Mary"} |        1 | 1       |    0 |
|   3 | {"name": "Pete"}         |      999 | 1       |    0 |
+-----+-------------------------+-----------+---------+------+
3 rows in set (0.00 sec)

mysql>
```

Example 6-11 -- JSON_TABLE() used with a DEFAULT value for missing data and EXISTS to determine if the data is available.

The above example shows how to deal with a missing value. By specifying DEFAULT '999' ON EMPTY, the server will return the default value when the desired key/value pair. The third record is missing a value for 'x' and the value 999 is inserted into the table.

The EXISTS keyword returns a Boolean answer if the referenced key/value pair exists. Since all the records have a 'name' key/value pair the hasname column reports a 1 in the hasname column. But not one of the records has a mojo key/value pair so a 0 is returned.

```
MySQL  localhost:33060+ ssl  test  SQL > SELECT * FROM t1,
                                      ->        JSON_TABLE(doc,"$" COLUMNS (
                                      ->        xHasValue INT PATH "$.x" DEFAULT '999' ON EMP
                                      ->        hasname CHAR(10) EXISTS PATH "$.name",
                                      ->        mojo CHAR(5) EXISTS PATH "$.mojo"))
                                      ->        AS t2
                                      ->        WHERE hasname=1 and xHasValue = 1;
+-----+---------------------------+-----------+---------+------+
| _id | doc                       | xHasValue | hasname | mojo |
+-----+---------------------------+-----------+---------+------+
|   1 | {"x": "1", "name": "Mary"}|         1 | 1       | 0    |
+-----+---------------------------+-----------+---------+------+
1 row in set (0.0007 sec)
MySQL  localhost:33060+ ssl  test  SQL >
```

```
mysql> SELECT * FROM t1,
       JSON_TABLE(doc,"$" COLUMNS (
       xHasValue INT PATH "$.x" DEFAULT '999' ON EMPTY,
       hasname CHAR(10) EXISTS PATH "$.name",
       mojo CHAR(5) EXISTS PATH "$.mojo"))
       AS t2
       WHERE hasname=1 and xHasValue = 1;
+-----+---------------------------+-----------+---------+------+
| _id | doc                       | xHasValue | hasname | mojo |
+-----+---------------------------+-----------+---------+------+
|   2 | {"x": 1, "name": "Mary"}  |         1 | 1       | 0    |
```

```
+-----+-------------------------+----------+---------+------+
```
1 row in set (0.01 sec)

Example 6-12 -- Using the Boolean data from JSON_TABLE()'s EXIST keyword as part of a query

Example 6-9 shows how to use the Boolean data from **JSON_TABLE()** in an SQL query, In this example the desired data has the hasname column equal to one and the xHasValue column equal to one. By using such queries it is very easy to determine if documents do indeed have certain key/value pairs.

Nested Data

JSON_TABLE() also has the ability to walk down the JSON document path and retrieve nested data. In the following example there are several values of z for each record's y key. The ability to extract each individual value comes from the **NESTED PATH** option.

```
MySQL  localhost:33060+ ssl  test  SQL > SELECT * FROM t2,
                                     -> JSON_TABLE(doc, "$" COLUMNS (
                                     -> myX INT PATH "$.x",
                                     ->         NESTED PATH "$.y[*]" COLUMNS (
                                     ->                 myID FOR ORDINALITY,
                                     ->                 myZ CHAR(10) PATH "$.z")))
                                     ->         AS tt;
+-----+------------------------------------------------+------+------+------+
| _id | doc                                            | myX  | myID | myZ  |
+-----+------------------------------------------------+------+------+------+
|  10 | {"x": 1, "y": [{"z": 1}, {"z": 3}]}            |   1  |   1  | 1    |
|  10 | {"x": 1, "y": [{"z": 1}, {"z": 3}]}            |   1  |   2  | 3    |
|  20 | {"x": 2, "y": [{"z": 2}, {"z": 4}]}            |   2  |   1  | 2    |
|  20 | {"x": 2, "y": [{"z": 2}, {"z": 4}]}            |   2  |   2  | 4    |
|  30 | {"x": 33, "y": [{"z": 2}, {"z": 3}, {"z": 4}]} |  33  |   1  | 2    |
|  30 | {"x": 33, "y": [{"z": 2}, {"z": 3}, {"z": 4}]} |  33  |   2  | 3    |
|  30 | {"x": 33, "y": [{"z": 2}, {"z": 3}, {"z": 4}]} |  33  |   3  | 4    |
+-----+------------------------------------------------+------+------+------+
7 rows in set (0.0006 sec)
MySQL  localhost:33060+ ssl  test  SQL >
```

```
mysql>SELECT * FROM t2,
        JSON_TABLE(doc, "$" COLUMNS (
            myX INT PATH "$.x",
            NESTED PATH "$.y[*]" COLUMNS (
                myID FOR ORDINALITY,
                myZ CHAR(10) PATH "$.z")))
            AS tt;
mysql> SELECT * FROM t2;
+-----+------------------------------------------------+
| _id | doc                                            |
+-----+------------------------------------------------+
|  10 | {"x": 1, "y": [{"z": 1}, {"z": 3}]}            |
|  20 | {"x": 2, "y": [{"z": 2}, {"z": 4}]}            |
|  30 | {"x": 33, "y": [{"z": 2}, {"z": 3}, {"z": 4}]} |
+-----+------------------------------------------------+
3 rows in set (0.02 sec)
```

Example 6-13 -- This name has nested values of key *z* within the key *y*.

The ability to extract all values of *z* from the *y* can be done with string handling functions or some very nasty regular expression code.   However **JSON_TABLE** allows walking down paths with nested values.

```
MySQL  localhost:33060+ ssl  test  SQL > SELECT * FROM t2,
                                      -> JSON_TABLE(doc, "$" COLUMNS (
                                      -> myX INT PATH "$.x",
                                      ->        NESTED PATH "$.y[*]" COLUMNS (
                                      ->              myID FOR ORDINALITY,
                                      ->              myZ CHAR(10) PATH "$.z")))
                                      ->        AS tt;
+------+----------------------------------------------+------+------+------+
| _id  | doc                                          | myX  | myID | myZ  |
+------+----------------------------------------------+------+------+------+
|  10  | {"x": 1, "y": [{"z": 1}, {"z": 3}]}          |  1   |  1   |  1   |
|  10  | {"x": 1, "y": [{"z": 1}, {"z": 3}]}          |  1   |  2   |  3   |
|  20  | {"x": 2, "y": [{"z": 2}, {"z": 4}]}          |  2   |  1   |  2   |
|  20  | {"x": 2, "y": [{"z": 2}, {"z": 4}]}          |  2   |  2   |  4   |
|  30  | {"x": 33, "y": [{"z": 2}, {"z": 3}, {"z": 4}]} |  33  |  1   |  2   |
|  30  | {"x": 33, "y": [{"z": 2}, {"z": 3}, {"z": 4}]} |  33  |  2   |  3   |
|  30  | {"x": 33, "y": [{"z": 2}, {"z": 3}, {"z": 4}]} |  33  |  3   |  4   |
+------+----------------------------------------------+------+------+------+
7 rows in set (0.0006 sec)
MySQL  localhost:33060+ ssl  test  SQL >
```

```
mysql> SELECT * FROM t2,
          JSON_TABLE(doc, "$" COLUMNS (
          myX INT PATH "$.x",
          NESTED PATH "$.y[*]" COLUMNS (
                  myID FOR ORDINALITY,
                  myZ CHAR(10) PATH "$.z")))
          AS tt;
+------+----------------------------------------------+------+------+------+
| _id  | doc                                          | myX  | myID | myZ  |
+------+----------------------------------------------+------+------+------+
|  10  | {"x": 1, "y": [{"z": 1}, {"z": 3}]}          |  1   |  1   |  1   |
|  10  | {"x": 1, "y": [{"z": 1}, {"z": 3}]}          |  1   |  2   |  3   |
```

```
| 20 | {"x": 2, "y": [{"z": 2}, {"z": 4}]}                | 2 | 1 | 2 |
| 20 | {"x": 2, "y": [{"z": 2}, {"z": 4}]}                | 2 | 2 | 4 |
| 30 | {"x": 33, "y": [{"z": 2}, {"z": 3}, {"z": 4}]} | 33 | 1 | 2 |
| 30 | {"x": 33, "y": [{"z": 2}, {"z": 3}, {"z": 4}]} | 33 | 2 | 3 |
| 30 | {"x": 33, "y": [{"z": 2}, {"z": 3}, {"z": 4}]} | 33 | 3 | 4 |
+-----+---------------------------------------------------+------+------+------+
7 rows in set (0.00 sec)

mysql>
```

Example 6-13 -- Using the NESTED PATH option with JSON_TABLE to extract all values of *z* from the *y* key/value pair. And JSON_TABLE() can also provide an ordinal number for returned data.

This may appear more confusing that it really is. It often helps to read the SQL statements aloud to help comprehension. In Example 6-11, the **NESTED PATH** of $.**y[*]** (also could have been **$.y** as well) is searched for any values of **z** in that path. Or, **y** becomes its own document and the server searched within it for any values of **z**.

The **FOR ORDINALITY** operator allows a running total for each of the values that are broken out in the **NESTED PATH** operation. The document with the *_id* of 10 has two ordinal values because there were two *z* values in that document's *y* key/value pair. And the document with the *_id* of 30 has three because its document has three values for *z* under the *y* key/value pair.

Chapter 7

Generated Columns

The MySQL server cannot index JSON columns. Generally you want indexes to be as small as practicable for speed and trying to use up to a gigabyte of unstructured data would not be efficient. This is similar to other data blobs. However, data from the JSON column can be extracted into a generated column and that column can be indexed.

There are two types of generated columns. The virtual generated column is evaluated when the column is read but before any triggers that may exist for that column. The stored generated column is evaluated and stored when data is either inserted or updated. The default is virtual and they can be mixed in a table together.

Virtual columns cannot contain subqueries, parameters, variables, stored functions, and user-defined functions. You cannot use the AUTO_INCREAMENT attribute in a virtual column or base a virtual column off a column that uses AUTO_INCREMENT. Foreign key constraints on a stored generated column cannot use ON UPDATE CASCADE, ON DELETE SET NULL, ON UPDATE SET NULL, ON DELETE SET DEFAULT, or ON UPDATE SET DEFAULT Also foreign key constraints cannot reference a virtual generated column. There

are several other constraints detailed at in the MySQL manual
that are worth noting at a later time.

Using Generated Columns

The keyword **AS** denotes a generated column. The following
example calculated the taxable amount of an item given the item
price and multiplied it by the tax rate.

```
MySQL  localhost:33060+ ssl  test  SQL > CREATE TABLE taxCalc (itemPrice DECIMAL(10,3),
                                      -> taxRate DECIMAL(10,3),
                                      -> taxAmount DECIMAL(10,3) AS (itemPrice * taxRate));
Query OK, 0 rows affected (0.0879 sec)
MySQL  localhost:33060+ ssl  test  SQL > INSERT INTO taxCalc (itemPrice, taxRate)
                                      ->        VALUES (10.0,0.08), (100.0,0.25);
Query OK, 2 rows affected (0.0241 sec)

Records: 2  Duplicates: 0  Warnings: 0
MySQL  localhost:33060+ ssl  test  SQL > SELECT * FROM taxCalc;
+-----------+----------+-----------+
| itemPrice | taxRate  | taxAmount |
+-----------+----------+-----------+
|    10.000 |    0.080 |     0.800 |
|   100.000 |    0.250 |    25.000 |
+-----------+----------+-----------+
2 rows in set (0.0008 sec)
MySQL  localhost:33060+ ssl  test  SQL >
```

```
mysql> CREATE TABLE taxCalc (itemPrice DECIMAL(10,3),
                   taxRate DECIMAL(10,3),
taxAmount DECIMAL(10,3) AS (itemPrice * taxRate));
Query OK, 0 rows affected (0.01 sec)


mysql> INSERT INTO taxCalc (itemPrice, taxRate)
       VALUES (10.0,0.08), (100.0,0.25);
Query OK, 2 rows affected (0.01 sec)
Records: 2  Duplicates: 0  Warnings: 0


mysql> SELECT * FROM taxCalc;
```

```
+-----------+----------+-----------+
| itemPrice | taxRate  | taxAmount |
+-----------+----------+-----------+
|    10.000 |   0.080  |    0.800  |
|   100.000 |   0.250  |   25.000  |
+-----------+----------+-----------+
2 rows in set (0.00 sec)

mysql>
```

Example 7-1 -- Using generated columns to calculate values. The taxRate is the percentage of the itemPrice to be taxed. The server calculates the taxAmount.

Note that only the itemPrice and taxRates were entered into the table and the server calculated the taxAmount column.

COLUMNs GENERATED FROM JSON

The *world_x countryinfo* table has a generated column and is a prime example of the MySQL Document Store table format. The InnoDB storage engine requires a PRIMARY KEY and will pick one, often poorly, if not specified. The MySQL server will create a column named **_id** when a collection is created and denote it as the primary key. If there is no **_id** data in the JSON document column named **doc** the column will hold a null.

```
MySQL  localhost:33060+ ssl  world_x  SQL > DESCRIBE countryinfo;
+--------+-------------+------+-----+---------+------------------+
| Field  | Type        | Null | Key | Default | Extra            |
+--------+-------------+------+-----+---------+------------------+
| doc    | json        | YES  |     | NULL    |                  |
| _id    | varchar(32) | NO   | PRI | NULL    | STORED GENERATED |
+--------+-------------+------+-----+---------+------------------+
2 rows in set (0.0034 sec)
MySQL  localhost:33060+ ssl  world_x  SQL >
```

```
mysql> DESC countryinfo;

+-------+-------------+------+-----+---------+------------------+
| Field | Type        | Null | Key | Default | Extra            |
+-------+-------------+------+-----+---------+------------------+
| doc   | json        | YES  |     | NULL    |                  |
| _id   | varchar(32) | NO   | PRI | NULL    | STORED GENERATED |
+-------+-------------+------+-----+---------+------------------+
2 rows in set (0.00 sec)

mysql>
```

**Example 7-2 -- How the MySQL Document Store creates
collections**

A simple DESCRIBE table will show us the layout of the
table and that there is a stored generated column but not the
actual code for the generation.

```
mysql> SHOW CREATE TABLE countryinfo;

+------------+-------------------------------------------------------------------
--------------------------------------------------------------------------------
-----------------------------------------------------------+
| Table      | Create Table
|
+------------+-------------------------------------------------------------------
--------------------------------------------------------------------------------
-----------------------------------------------------------+
| countryinfo | CREATE TABLE `countryinfo` (
  `doc` json DEFAULT NULL,
  `_id` varchar(32) GENERATED ALWAYS AS (json_unquote(json_extract(`doc`,_utf8'$._id')))
STORED NOT NULL,
  PRIMARY KEY (`_id`)
) ENGINE=InnoDB DEFAULT CHARSET=utf8 |
+------------+-------------------------------------------------------------------
--------------------------------------------------------------------------------
-----------------------------------------------------------+
1 row in set (0.00 sec)
```

Example 7-3 -- More details on the Document Store's table

But a SHOW CREATE TABLE provides the details on the generation of the created table. It is easy to see that the _id column is created from JSON column doc's key/value pair of _id. And note the UTF8 casting of this field.

Any other JSON key (or keys in combination - check the MySQL manual for Composite Indexes) can be used in a generated column. In cases where you are regularly extracting one key/value pair it may be faster to use a generated column and index that generated column to search via SQL.

```
MySQL  localhost:33060+ ssl  world_x  SQL > ALTER TABLE countryinfo
                                     ->        ADD COLUMN PopulationCountry INT AS
                                     ->        (JSON_UNQUOTE(doc->"$.demographics.Population"));
Query OK, 0 rows affected (0.0649 sec)

Records: 0  Duplicates: 0  Warnings: 0
MySQL  localhost:33060+ ssl  world_x  SQL >
```

mysql> **ALTER TABLE countryinfo**

   ADD COLUMN PopulationCountry INT AS

   (JSON_UNQUOTE(doc->"$.demographics.Population"));

Query OK, 0 rows affected (0.25 sec)

Records: 0 Duplicates: 0 Warnings: 0

Example 7-4 -- Using ALTER TABLE to add generated column for Population.

But there are two types of virtual columns and it is better to use the STORED option for building indexes. The virtual type is not stored and must be computers at access which is a lot of work which is best left to the stored type where the value is materialized in a column that is stored when the data is written. If the table is examined after Example 7-3, it is easy to see that the new column is VIRTUAL and not stored.

```
MySQL  localhost:33060+ ssl  world_x  SQL > DESC countryinfo;
+------------------+-------------+------+-----+---------+-------------------+
| Field            | Type        | Null | Key | Default | Extra             |
+------------------+-------------+------+-----+---------+-------------------+
| doc              | json        | YES  |     | NULL    |                   |
| _id              | varchar(32) | NO   | PRI | NULL    | STORED GENERATED  |
| PopulationCountry | int        | YES  |     | NULL    | VIRTUAL GENERATED |
+------------------+-------------+------+-----+---------+-------------------+
3 rows in set (0.0033 sec)
MySQL  localhost:33060+ ssl  world_x  SQL >
```

mysql> **DESC countryinfo;**

+------------------+------------+------+-----+---------+------------------+

```
| Field             | Type        | Null | Key | Default | Extra             |
+-------------------+-------------+------+-----+---------+-------------------+
| doc               | json        | YES  |     | NULL    |                   |
| _id               | varchar(32) | NO   | PRI | NULL    | STORED GENERATED  |
| PopulationCountry | int(11)     | YES  |     | NULL    | VIRTUAL GENERATED |
+-------------------+-------------+------+-----+---------+-------------------+
3 rows in set (0.06 sec)

mysql>
```

Example 7-5 -- The description of *countryinfo* shows the generated column setup in Example 7-4 shows it is a VIRTUAL generated column which is not what is desired.

Luckily it is easy to remove the new columns using ALTER table (**ALTER TABLE countryinfo DROP COLUMN PopulationCountry**) and then reissue the command to create the generated column but this time with the keyword STORED appended. And checking the description shows that the new Population column is indeed a STORED generated column.

```
MySQL  localhost:33060+ ssl  world_x  SQL > alter table countryinfo drop column PopulationCountry;
Query OK, 0 rows affected (0.3316 sec)

Records: 0  Duplicates: 0  Warnings: 0
MySQL  localhost:33060+ ssl  world_x  SQL > ALTER TABLE countryinfo
                                         -> ADD COLUMN PopulationCountry INT AS
                                         -> (JSON_UNQUOTE(doc->"$.demographics.Population"))
                                         -> STORED;
Query OK, 239 rows affected (0.2848 sec)

Records: 239  Duplicates: 0  Warnings: 0
MySQL  localhost:33060+ ssl  world_x  SQL >
MySQL  localhost:33060+ ssl  world_x  SQL > DESC countryinfo;
+-------------------+-------------+------+-----+---------+------------------+
| Field             | Type        | Null | Key | Default | Extra            |
+-------------------+-------------+------+-----+---------+------------------+
| doc               | json        | YES  |     | NULL    |                  |
| _id               | varchar(32) | NO   | PRI | NULL    | STORED GENERATED |
| PopulationCountry | int         | YES  |     | NULL    | STORED GENERATED |
+-------------------+-------------+------+-----+---------+------------------+
3 rows in set (0.0027 sec)
MySQL  localhost:33060+ ssl  world_x  SQL >
```

```
mysql> ALTER TABLE countryinfo
    DROP COLUMN PopulationCountry;
mysql> ALTER TABLE countryinfo
    ADD COLUMN PopulationCountry INT AS
(JSON_UNQUOTE(doc->"$.demographics.Population")) STORED;
Query OK, 239 rows affected (0.19 sec)
Records: 239  Duplicates: 0  Warnings: 0

mysql> desc countryinfo;
+-------------------+-------------+------+-----+---------+-----------------+
| Field             | Type        | Null | Key | Default | Extra           |
+-------------------+-------------+------+-----+---------+-----------------+
| doc               | json        | YES  |     | NULL    |                 |
| _id               | varchar(32) | NO   | PRI | NULL    | STORED GENERATED |
| PopulationCountry | int(11)     | YES  |     | NULL    | STORED GENERATED |
+-------------------+-------------+------+-----+---------+-----------------+
3 rows in set (0.00 sec)
```

Example 7-6 -- The description of countryinfo now shows the desired STORED GENERATED Population column.

There is still one more step needed in order to have an SQL usable index on the new column that will be something along the lines of CREATE **INDEX Population_Index on countryinfo (Population);** following the index naming convention of choice.

Chapter 8 - GeoJSON

MySQL 5.7 had several new features besides the JSON data type and included among them was a vast improvement in Graphical Information System support. MySQL follows the Open Geospatial Consortium OpenGIS® *Implementation Standard for Geographic information - Simple feature access - Part 2: SQL option* that proposes several to extend an SQL RDBMS to support spatial data. And MySQL also features functions for converting between spatial values and JSON and follows 1.0 specification of the GeoJSON standard found at <u>https://geojon.com</u>. GeoJSON supports the same geometric and geographic data types as MySQL.

ST_GeomFromGeoJSON

The **ST_GeomFromGeoJSON()** function process as GeoJSON formatted string and returns a geometry. There is a second optional argument on how to handle GeoJSON documents that contain geometries with coordinate dimensions higher than 2 a this option can have the value of 1 (default) reject the JSON formatted document and produce an error message, and 2,3,or 4 accept the document and strip off the coordinates for higher coordinate dimensions. And there is a third and final argument for the **SRID (Spatial Reference system Identifier)** argument, if given, must be a 32-bit unsigned integer. If not given, the geometry return value has an SRID of 4326.

Flag Value	Meaning
0	No options. This is the default
1	A bounding box is added to the output.
2	A short-format CRS URN is added to the output. The default format is the short format (EPSG:*srid*).
4	A long-format CRS URN (urn:ogc:def:crs:EPSG::*srid*) is added to the output . This flag overrides flag 2. Option values of 5 and 7 mean the same (a bounding box and a long-format CRS URN).

```
mysql> SELECT ST_AsText(ST_GeomFromGeoJSON('{ "type" :
"Point", "coordinates" : [99.1, 1.1]}'));
+-----------------------------------------------------------------------------+
| ST_AsText(ST_GeomFromGeoJSON('{ "type" : "Point", "coordinates" : [99.1, 1.1]}')) |
+-----------------------------------------------------------------------------+
| POINT(1.1 99.1)                                                             |
+-----------------------------------------------------------------------------+
1 row in set (0.01 sec)

mysql>
```

Example 8-1 -- Using ST_GeomFromGeoJSON

The **ST_AsGeoJSON()** function takes a JSON formatted string and turns it into a geometry. Note the wrapping of this function with **ST_AsText** to format the output to something more readable. The following without the **ST_AsText** displays its usefulness.

```
MySQL  localhost:33060+ ssl  world_x  SQL > SELECT
                      -> ST_GeomFromGeoJSON('{ "type" : "Point", "coordinates" : [99.1, 1.1]}',4);
+-------------------------------------------------------------------------+
| ST_GeomFromGeoJSON('{ "type" : "Point", "coordinates" : [99.1, 1.1]}',4) |
+-------------------------------------------------------------------------+
| ◆▨ ▨▨  fffff◆X@◆◆◆◆◆◆◆?                                            |
+-------------------------------------------------------------------------+
1 row in set (0.0006 sec)
MySQL  localhost:33060+ ssl  world_x  SQL >
```

```
mysql> SELECT  ST_GeomFromGeoJSON('{ "type" : "Point",
"coordinates" : [99.1, 1.1]}',4));
+-----------------------------------------------------------------------+
| ST_GeomFromGeoJSON('{ "type" : "Point", "coordinates" : [99.1, 1.1]}',4) |
+-----------------------------------------------------------------------+
| ◆       fffff◆X@◆◆◆◆◆◆◆?                                          |
+-----------------------------------------------------------------------+
1 row in set (0.00 sec)

mysql>
```

Example 8-2 -- Not exactly what was wanted from ST_GeomFromGeoJSON

ST_AsGeoJSON

The **ST_AsGeoJSON()** function is the opposite of **STGeomFromGeoJSON** in that it takes a geometry and produces a GeoJSON object. It has a first option of the number of decimal digits for coordinates. And options can be added as seen below to modify the output.

113

```
MySQL  localhost:33060+ ssl  world_x  SQL > SELECT
                            -> ST_AsGeoJSON(ST_GeomFromText('POINT(12.3456 23.4567)'),2);
+----------------------------------------------------------+
| ST_AsGeoJSON(ST_GeomFromText('POINT(12.3456 23.4567)'),2) |
+----------------------------------------------------------+
| {"type": "Point", "coordinates": [12.35, 23.46]}         |
+----------------------------------------------------------+
1 row in set (0.0003 sec)
MySQL  localhost:33060+ ssl  world_x  SQL >
```

mysql> **SELECT**

ST_AsGeoJSON(ST_GeomFromText('POINT(12.3456 23.4567)'),2);

```
+----------------------------------------------------------+
| ST_AsGeoJSON(ST_GeomFromText('POINT(12.3456 23.4567)'),2) |
+----------------------------------------------------------+
| {"type": "Point", "coordinates": [12.35, 23.46]}         |
+----------------------------------------------------------+
1 row in set (0.00 sec)
```

Example 8-3 -- Using STGeomFromGeoJSON

The options are a bitmask which means they can be combined. With no option the output as in the above.

Option Value	Meaning
1	Reject the document and produce an error. This is the default.
2, 3, 4	Accept the document, stripping off the coordinates at higher coordinate dimensions.

```
MySQL  localhost:33060+ ssl  world_x  SQL > SELECT
                            -> ST_AsGeoJSON(ST_GeomFromText('POINT(12.3456 23.4567)'),2,
+----------------------------------------------------------------+
| ST_AsGeoJSON(ST_GeomFromText('POINT(12.3456 23.4567)'),2,1)     |
+----------------------------------------------------------------+
| {"bbox": [12.35, 23.46, 12.35, 23.46], "type": "Point", "coordinates": [12.35, 23.46]} |
+----------------------------------------------------------------+
1 row in set (0.0006 sec)
MySQL  localhost:33060+ ssl  world_x  SQL >
```

```
mysql> SELECT ST_AsGeoJSON(ST_GeomFromText('POINT(12.3456
23.4567)'),2,1);
+--------------------------------------------------------------------------------
+
| ST_AsGeoJSON(ST_GeomFromText('POINT(12.3456 23.4567)'),2,1)
|
+--------------------------------------------------------------------------------
+
| {"bbox": [12.35, 23.46, 12.35, 23.46], "type": "Point", "coordinates": [12.35, 23.46]}
|
+--------------------------------------------------------------------------------
+
1 row in set (0.00 sec)
```

Example 8-4 -- ST_GeomFromText without options

Option 1 adds a bounding box (bbox) which is easy to see in
the above example. Option 2 adds a short-format CRS URN to the
output with default format being a short format (EPSG:srid).
Option 4 adds a long-format CRS URN (urn:ogc:def:crs:EPSG::srid)
and overrides option 2. Since this option field is a bitmask the
various options can be combined, option 3 is Option 1 plus
Option 2.

```
mysql> SELECT
ST_AsGeoJSON(ST_GeomFromText('POINT(12.3456
23.4567)'),2,4);
```

```
+----------------------------------------------------------+
| ST_AsGeoJSON(ST_GeomFromText('POINT(12.3456 23.4567)'),2,4) |
+----------------------------------------------------------+
| {"type": "Point", "coordinates": [12.35, 23.46]}          |
+----------------------------------------------------------+
1 row in set (0.00 sec)
```

mysql> **SELECT**

ST_AsGeoJSON(ST_GeomFromText('POINT(12.3456
23.4567)'),2,5);

```
+--------------------------------------------------------------------------------+
| ST_AsGeoJSON(ST_GeomFromText('POINT(12.3456 23.4567)'),2,5)                     |
+--------------------------------------------------------------------------------+
| {"bbox": [12.35, 23.46, 12.35, 23.46], "type": "Point", "coordinates": [12.35, 23.46]} |
+--------------------------------------------------------------------------------+
1 row in set (0.00 sec)
```

Example 8-5 -- Other options for the ST_GeoJSON
function

Chapter 9

PHP's JSON Functions

PHP is a very popular programming language that is the core of up to eighty percent of the Internet and has its own JSON functions. The question for developers is how to take advantage of what PHP offers for JSON and how to best use that with what MySQL offers. PHP's JSON functions require UTF8MB4 encoded strings.

JSON_DECODE

The **JSON_DECODE** function is used to convert a JSON formatted string and convert into a PHP variable. The MySQL JSON functions have no analog

Format **mixed json_decode (string $json [, bool $assoc = false [, int $depth = 512 [, int $options = 0]]])**

The first argument is the JSON formatted string to be decoded. The second is a Boolean value (true or false) to set the returned data into an associative array. The third argument is a recursive depth limit, one or greater. The fourth and final argument has two settable options:

JSON_OBJECT_AS_ARRAY has the same effect as setting assoc to TRUE and JSON_BIGINT_AS_STRING casts big integers to string instead of the default float.

```php
<?php

$json_string='{"name":"Dave","height":1.95,"c":[1,2,3]}';

var_dump(json_decode($json_string));          // Object output
var_dump(json_decode($json_string,true));    // Associative array
?>
```

Example 9-1 -- Simple PHP program to explore the PHP function json_decode

```
php j1.php
object(stdClass)#1 (3) {
  ["name"]=>
  string(4) "Dave"
  ["height"]=>
  float(1.95)
  ["c"]=>
  array(3) {
    [0]=>
    int(1)
    [1]=>
    int(2)
    [2]=>
    int(3)
  }
}
array(3) {
  ["name"]=>
```

```
    string(4) "Dave"
    ["height"]=>
    float(1.95)
    ["c"]=>
    array(3) {
      [0]=>
      int(1)
      [1]=>
      int(2)
      [2]=>
      int(3)
    }
  }
```

Example 9-2 Output of sample PHP program from example 9-1

JSON_ENCODE

The json_encode function turns values of variables into JSON strings.

string json_encode (mixed $value [, int $options = 0 [, int $depth = 512]])

```
Chapter 10
```

Loading JSON Data

There are many JSON datasets available but sometimes they are problematic to feed into a database. The first example will be a list of US Postal or Zip codes found at http://jsonstudio.com/resources/ and it is free of cost. Oftentimes at the start of a new programming project, a developer will be provided with some sample data that needs to be shoehorned onto the server, usually with little guidance other than 'just get it on the server'. This chapter will deal with some examples of just how to do that.

There are also several options for loading data including the bulk loader in the MySQL Shell that can work with parallel threads for extremely fast uploading. This chapter will loot at the non MySQL shell options first.

Building a .sql File for Loading

Step 1 -- Examine the data

The data for this example is supplied in a file named **zips.zip** and is unpacked by using the unzip command, **unzip zips.zip**. This will produce a file named **zips.json**.

```
$ head zips.json
```

{ "city" : "AGAWAM", "loc" : [-72.622739, 42.070206],
"pop" : 15338, "state" : "MA", "_id" : "01001" }
{ "city" : "CUSHMAN", "loc" : [-72.51564999999999,
42.377017], "pop" : 36963, "state" : "MA", "_id" : "01002"
}
{ "city" : "BARRE", "loc" : [-72.10835400000001, 42.409698
], "pop" : 4546, "state" : "MA", "_id" : "01005" }
{ "city" : "BELCHERTOWN", "loc" : [-72.41095300000001,
42.275103], "pop" : 10579, "state" : "MA", "_id" : "01007"
}
{ "city" : "BLANDFORD", "loc" : [-72.936114, 42.182949],
"pop" : 1240, "state" : "MA", "_id" : "01008" }
{ "city" : "BRIMFIELD", "loc" : [-72.188455, 42.116543],
"pop" : 3706, "state" : "MA", "_id" : "01010" }
{ "city" : "CHESTER", "loc" : [-72.988761, 42.279421],
"pop" : 1688, "state" : "MA", "_id" : "01011" }
{ "city" : "CHESTERFIELD", "loc" : [-72.833309, 42.38167
], "pop" : 177, "state" : "MA", "_id" : "01012" }
{ "city" : "CHICOPEE", "loc" : [-72.607962, 42.162046],
"pop" : 23396, "state" : "MA", "_id" : "01013" }
{ "city" : "CHICOPEE", "loc" : [-72.576142, 42.176443],
"pop" : 31495, "state" : "MA", "_id" : "01020" }

Example 10 -1 -- Examining the first rows of the zips,json datafile

The file contains almost 30,000 lines with one record per line. Before loading all those liens into the server, it helps to determine some of the use of that information. For illustration purposes, pretend what is desired of the data is

that a user could enter a five digit postal code and have
returned a city and state values. Also a user could enter a city
and state set of values and receive the zip code.

But what does the data provide to us? There are fields for
city, *loc*, *pop*, *state*, and *_id* (which is the zipcode itself).
It makes sense to use *_id* as a primary key.

Step 2 -- Create the Table

```
MySQL  localhost:33060+ ssl  world_x  SQL > use test;
Default schema set to 'test'.
Fetching table and column names from 'test' for auto-completion... Press ^C to stop.
MySQL  localhost:33060+ ssl  test  SQL > create table zipcode (doc JSON,
                         -> _id char(5) GENERATED ALWAYS AS (JSON_UNQUOTE(JSON_EXTRACT(doc,'$._id'))) STORED NOT NULL,
                         ->     PRIMARY KEY (_id));
Query OK, 0 rows affected (0.0810 sec)
MySQL  localhost:33060+ ssl  test  SQL >
```

mysql> **use test;**

Database changed

mysql> **create table zipcode (doc JSON,**

    _id char(5) GENERATED ALWAYS AS

(JSON_UNQUOTE(JSON_EXTRACT(doc,'$._id'))) STORED NOT NULL,

    PRIMARY KEY (_id));

Query OK, 0 rows affected (0.03 sec)

mysql>

Example 10 - 2 -- Creating a table for the JSON data

The postal codes are five places in length and many have
leading zeros. MySQL's Integer fields will drop leading zeros

but CHAR fields will not. And in this case the leading zeros
need to be retained as they are important.

Step 3 -- Load the Data Using a Wrapper

Data often needs some tinkering to allow it to be imported
into a database, even a schema less database. What is needed
here is a way to wrap each line of data into a SQL INSERT
statement. This can be done with a very simple BASH script


```
#!/bin/bash
file="/home/dstokes/Downloads/zips.json"
while IFS= read line
do
     echo "INSERT INTO zipcode (doc) VALUES ('$line');"
done <"$file"
```


**Example 10 - 3 -- Script file to wrap the individual
lines of the zips.json file with a SQL statement**

This script reads the data from the zips.json file, line by
line, and then echoes the content wrapped in a SQL statement.
This script can have its output piped to a MySQL session or sent
to a file as seen below.


```
./loader.sh > foo
```


**Example 10-4 -- Using the script from the previous
example to create a file with the generated SQL statements.**

It is easy to see in the next example that the data is now in a proper format for inserting into the database.

```
$head foo
INSERT INTO zipcode (doc) VALUES ('{ "city" : "AGAWAM", "loc" : [ -72.622739,
42.070206 ], "pop" : 15338, "state" : "MA", "_id" : "01001" }');
INSERT INTO zipcode (doc) VALUES ('{ "city" : "CUSHMAN", "loc" : [ -
72.51564999999999, 42.377017 ], "pop" : 36963, "state" : "MA", "_id" : "01002"
}');
INSERT INTO zipcode (doc) VALUES ('{ "city" : "BARRE", "loc" : [ -
72.10835400000001, 42.409698 ], "pop" : 4546, "state" : "MA", "_id" : "01005"
}');
INSERT INTO zipcode (doc) VALUES ('{ "city" : "BELCHERTOWN", "loc" : [ -
72.41095300000001, 42.275103 ], "pop" : 10579, "state" : "MA", "_id" : "01007"
}');
INSERT INTO zipcode (doc) VALUES ('{ "city" : "BLANDFORD", "loc" : [ -
72.936114, 42.182949 ], "pop" : 1240, "state" : "MA", "_id" : "01008" }');
INSERT INTO zipcode (doc) VALUES ('{ "city" : "BRIMFIELD", "loc" : [ -
72.188455, 42.116543 ], "pop" : 3706, "state" : "MA", "_id" : "01010" }');
INSERT INTO zipcode (doc) VALUES ('{ "city" : "CHESTER", "loc" : [ -72.988761,
42.279421 ], "pop" : 1688, "state" : "MA", "_id" : "01011" }');
INSERT INTO zipcode (doc) VALUES ('{ "city" : "CHESTERFIELD", "loc" : [ -
72.833309, 42.38167 ], "pop" : 177, "state" : "MA", "_id" : "01012" }');
INSERT INTO zipcode (doc) VALUES ('{ "city" : "CHICOPEE", "loc" : [ -72.607962,
42.162046 ], "pop" : 23396, "state" : "MA", "_id" : "01013" }');
INSERT INTO zipcode (doc) VALUES ('{ "city" : "CHICOPEE", "loc" : [ -72.576142,
42.176443 ], "pop" : 31495, "state" : "MA", "_id" : "01020" }');
```

Example 10-4 -- The output of the shell script can be seen here. This example only shows the first several lines after transformation

Finally the data is loaded with a simple **mysql -u root -p test < foo** command.

Step 4 -- Double Check the Data

At this point the data needs some quality control check. A good place to start is with the first record in the data file to see if the data is complete.

```
mysql> select * from zipcode where _id = '01001';
+--------------------------------------------------------------------------------+-------+
| doc                                                                            | _id   |
+--------------------------------------------------------------------------------+-------+
| {"_id": "01001", "loc": [-72.622739, 42.070206], "pop": 15338, "city": "AGAWAM", "state": "MA"} | 01001 |
+--------------------------------------------------------------------------------+-------+
1 row in set (0.00 sec)
```

Example 10--5 -- Examining a known good example from the database. For Zip Code leading zeros are important and must be retained so checking for an example with a leading zero assures that was completed correctly.

It is an easy comparison to look at the first line in both the raw data and the foo file to ensure they have the same data. Then the data in the database table can be checked. This check also provides a way to check that the leading zero for the *_id* field has not been stripped (it would have had an INT been used instead of a CHAR data type).

But what about looking up a zipcode given a *city* and a *state*? That currently is a challenge.

```
mysql> SELECT _id FROM zipcode
        WHERE JSON_EXTRACT(doc,"$.city") = "LEMON GROVE"
        AND
        JSON_EXTRACT(doc,"$.state") = "CA";
```

```
+-------+
| _id   |
+-------+
| 91945 |
+-------+
1 row in set (0.02 sec)
```

Example 10-6 -- Finding the zip/postal code given the _state_ and _city_ fields

There are many other validations that can be done on the information to spot check the validity of the information but the first tests are good. From this point other steps could be done to ease access of the data such as generated columns, views, stored procedures, or indexes on the data for future queries that are known to be desired at this point in development.

JQ -- JSON CLI Parser

Another option is the _jq_ is a lightweight and flexible command-line JSON processor. THis processor acts much like _sed_ in that it allows you to slice, filter, map, and transform data from one format to another. For instance it can be used to convert JSON data into CSV (comma separated values) for loading into a non-JSON column MySQL database. It can be downloaded from https://stedolan.github.io/jq/ and there is an online version at https://jqplay.org/ for experimentation. Plus _jq_ uses the PCRE regular expression parser as many other languages. This wonderful tool deserves to have much more written about it than the simple examples here and reading the manual is a quick way to become acquainted with the many features of this tool.

With No Arguments

```
$ head -2 zips.json | jq
{
  "city": "AGAWAM",
  "loc": [
    -72.622739,
    42.070206
  ],
  "pop": 15338,
  "state": "MA",
  "_id": "01001"
}
{
  "city": "CUSHMAN",
  "loc": [
    -72.51565,
    42.377017
  ],
  "pop": 36963,
  "state": "MA",
  "_id": "01002"
}
```

Example 10-7 -- Using *jq* without arguments will 'pretty print' the JSON document.

With no arguments to jq it will 'pretty print' the JSON document. This is extremely handy for extremely complex documents with many layers of embedded objects and arrays that are hard to view with on a single flat line.

Selecting Certain Fields

There will be occasions when not all the data in a JSON document will be of interest and jq can be used to reform the data to provide only selected parts.

```
$ head -2 zips.json | jq '{city, state, _id}'
{
  "city": "AGAWAM",
  "state": "MA",
  "_id": "01001"
}
{
  "city": "CUSHMAN",
  "state": "MA",
  "_id": "01002"
}
```

Example 10 -- 8 -- Using *jq* to output only some of the data from the source JSON document.

```
$ head -2 zips.json | jq '{(.city): .state, _id}'
{
```

```
  "AGAWAM": "MA",
  "_id": "01001"
}
{
  "CUSHMAN": "MA",
  "_id": "01002"
}
```

Example 10 -9 -- Modifying the data to convert a key into a value.

In the above example the value of the *city* key was converted into a value. Then that new key was given the value of the *state* key/value pair. The flexibility of *jq* can be a great asset.

The Restaurant Collection

MongoDB was proven to be a popular NoSQL document store and one of their example datasets is known as the restaurant collection. It is 25,359 lines of restaurant data that is a good example for showing how to load data into MySQL. The entire collection can be downloaded from the URL in Appendix B.

First thing to notice is that there is no *_id* key/value pair unlike the **zipcode** example. There is however a *restaurant_id* key/value pair that is unique for all the record. With InnoDB tables it helps to have a primary key index of your choice. So the *restaurant_id* is an easy choice for use as a primary key.

Each line of this collection is a JSON object, bounded by curly braces. Using a script similar to Example 10-3 to load the data is a good idea however this is a problem in the data.

Many of the records have apostrophes in the restaurant name which will cause those records to fail with a SQL error; anything after the second apostrophe fails the syntax checker. What needs to be done is to change the single quote (') to either a double single quote ('') which the server interprets as an properly escaped single quote in the middle of a literal. There are many ways of doing this including using a favorite text editor. But large source files may be beyond the size that text editors itself of the system can handle. Linux users can use a stream editor like sed. One the single quotes are turned to double single quotes, the data can be fed into the server as in Example 10-4.

```
INSERT INTO restaurant (doc) values ('{"address":
{"building": "1924", "coord":
[-73.9483236, 40.6387106], "street": "Nostrand Avenue",
"zipcode": "11226"}, "bo
rough": "Brooklyn", "cuisine": "Chinese", "grades":
[{"date": {"$date": 14143680
00000}, "grade": "A", "score": 7}, {"date": {"$date":
1384732800000}, "grade": "
A", "score": 7}, {"date": {"$date": 1362528000000},
"grade": "B", "score": 16},
{"date": {"$date": 1340668800000}, "grade": "A", "score":
9}, {"date": {"$date":
```

```
1326153600000}, "grade": "A", "score": 10}], "name":
"Kenny'S Restaurant", "res
taurant_id": "40919894"}');
```

**Example 10-10 – Using the earlier method to load data
will fail on some records as there are embedded apostrophes in
the restaurant names and in the above the bold italic ends where
the MySQL Syntax checking will see the end of the SQL query.
What is needed is to change *Kenny's Restaurant* to *Kenny''s
Restaurant* as the MySQL server will correctly escape the
apostrophe in the name.**

One of the many commands that could be used is *sed*. The
sed utility is a stream editor from the early days of the Unix
operating system. It is easy to tell it to search for the single
– single quote and turn it into two single quotes.

```
sed "s/'/''/g" primer-dataset.json > updated.json
```

**Example 10-11 – Here sed is used to convert single –
single quotes to double single quotes.**

Now we can use updated data with the loader script to
create a table to feed to the database. This type of data
cleaning is typical of what is needed to load third party data
into a database server.

```
mysql> SELECT _id,
            JSON_PRETTY(doc)
        FROM restaurant
```

```
        LIMIT 1\G
*********************** 1. row
***********************
        _id: 30075445
JSON_PRETTY(doc): {
  "name": "Morris Park Bake Shop",
  "grades": [
    {
      "date": {
        "$date": 1393804800000
      },
      "grade": "A",
      "score": 2
    },
    {
      "date": {
        "$date": 1378857600000
      },
      "grade": "A",
      "score": 6
    },
    {
      "date": {
        "$date": 1358985600000
      },
      "grade": "A",
      "score": 10
    },
    {
      "date": {
        "$date": 1322006400000
      },
```

```
        "grade": "A",
        "score": 9
      },
      {
        "date": {
          "$date": 1299715200000
        },
        "grade": "B",
        "score": 14
      }
    ],
    "address": {
      "coord": [
        -73.856077,
        40.848447
      ],
      "street": "Morris Park Ave",
      "zipcode": "10462",
      "building": "1007"
    },
    "borough": "Bronx",
    "cuisine": "Bakery",
    "restaurant_id": "30075445"
}
1 row in set (0.00 sec)

mysql>
```

Example 10-12 – An example record after the data has been cleaned up and then fed into the server.

The MySQL Shell JSON and Bulk Loaders

The MySQL Shell also known as mysqlsh provides a way to upload data into a MySQL instance into a relational table or a JSON document collection. JSON documents are examined to see if they are properly formatted before inserting them into the target database. This is much faster than writing a script to use multiple INSERT statements.

The ability to import data in parallel is a feature of the MySQL Shell. And you can run it from a command line instead of from within an interactive shell.

util.importJson And util.import_json

The mysqlsh program has three conversational modes - SQL, Python, and JavaScript. The JSON importer is not available under SQL mode but can be found in JS (JavaScript Mode as util.importJSON and in Python as util.import_json. For clarity the JavaScript name of importJSON will be used.

Format: util.importJSon(file[, options])

```
 MySQL  localhost:33060+ ssl  world_x  JS >
util.importJson("C:/Users/dstokes/Downloads/dave.txt")
Importing from file "C:/Users/dstokes/Downloads/dave.txt" to collection `world_x`.`dave` in MySQL
Server at localhost:33060

.. 1

Processed 40 bytes in 1 document in 0.2346 sec (1.00 document/s)
Total successfully imported documents 1 (1.00 document/s)
 MySQL  localhost:33060+ ssl  world_x  JS > \sql
```

```
Switching to SQL mode... Commands end with ;
 MySQL  localhost:33060+ ssl  world_x  SQL > select * from dave\G
*************************** 1. row ***************************
        doc: {"_id": "00005edf7ed50000000000000001", "name": "Dave", "Location": "Texas"}
        _id: 00005edf7ed50000000000000001
_json_schema: {"type": "object"}
1 row in set (0.0005 sec)
```

Example 10-13 - A very simple JSON document is loaded with the util.importJSON() utility from the Downloads directory of a Windows PC and stored in a SQL schema that is compatible with the MySQL Document Store.

Example 10-13 shows a very simple example of the use of this utility without options. The file dave.txt contained the JSON document { "name" : "Dave", "Location" : "Texas" }. During the upload the server added the **_id** column (please see description in chapter on the MySQL Document Store) and the **_json_schema** column.

This utility also supports converting BSON data types found in MongoDB into MySQL values.

```
 MySQL  localhost:33060+ ssl  world_x  JS >
util.importJson("c:/users/dstokes/downloads/dave.txt",{ "schema"
: "demo"})
Importing from file "c:/users/dstokes/downloads/dave.txt" to
collection `demo`.`dave` in MySQL Server at localhost:33060

.. 1
Processed 40 bytes in 1 document in 0.0067 sec (1.00 document/s)
Total successfully imported documents 1 (1.00 document/s)
```

```
 MySQL  localhost:33060+ ssl  world_x  JS >
util.importJson("c:/users/dstokes/downloads/dave.txt",{ "schema"
: "demo", "collection" : "xyz"})
Importing from file "c:/users/dstokes/downloads/dave.txt" to
collection `demo`.`xyz` in MySQL Server at localhost:33060


.. 1
Processed 40 bytes in 1 document in 0.0112 sec (1.00 document/s)
Total successfully imported documents 1 (1.00 document/s)
 MySQL  localhost:33060+ ssl  world_x  JS >
util.importJson("c:/users/dstokes/downloads/dave.txt",{ "schema"
: "demo", "table" : "xyz2"})
Importing from file "c:/users/dstokes/downloads/dave.txt" to
table `demo`.`xyz2` in MySQL Server at localhost:33060


.. 1
Processed 40 bytes in 1 document in 0.0068 sec (1.00 document/s)
Total successfully imported documents 1 (1.00 document/s)
MySQL  localhost:33060+ ssl  world_x  JS >
util.importJson("c:/users/dstokes/downloads/dave.txt",{ "schema"
: "demo", "table" : "xyz3", "tableColumn" : "mydoc"})
Importing from file "c:/users/dstokes/downloads/dave.txt" to
table `demo`.`xyz3` in MySQL Server at localhost:33060


.. 1
Processed 40 bytes in 1 document in 0.0078 sec (1.00 document/s)
Total successfully imported documents 1 (1.00 document/s)
```

**Example 13-14 -- Various options can be specified with
an JSON document to tailor how loadJson handles the data.**

Example 13-14 shows how the options can be added to effect how the data is loaded. The various options and arguments are enclosed in a JSON document, i.e. **{ "schema" : "demo", "table" : "xyz3", "tableColumn" : "mydoc"}**.

loadJson Options

The options dictionary supports the following options:

- schema: string - name of target schema to be used to store the data. If a schema name is not provided, MySQL Shell attempts to identify and use the schema name in use in the current session. And if the schema name is not specified and cannot be identified from the session, an error is returned.

- collection: string - name of collection where the data will be imported. Note that you can specify the name of a collection or a table but not both. The collection will be created is it does not exist using the name specified.

Note that the loadJSON utility will default to using or creating a target collection with the name of the file, without file extension, from the of the file where the data is drawn from if a collection, table, or tableColumn is not provided.

- table: string - name of table where the data will be imported. Note that you can specify the name of a collection or a table but not both. If the table does not exist it will be created.

- tableColumn: is the name of the column where to place the imported JSON data and the default is `doc ` if left unspecified. And will work with tables only not collections. If the table exists you must use the name of an existing column as the utility will not issue an ALTER TABLE to add the new column. Not specifying a column name will result in the default `doc` column being used. Specifying the tableColumn option but omitting the table option results in the name of the supplied import file, without the file extension, being used as the table name. The tableColumn implies the use of the table option and cannot be combined with the collection option.

- convertBsonTypes: Set to true to convert BSON data toa a MySQL format. The default is false. When you specified as convertBsonTypes: true, each of the represented BSON types is converted to a MySQL representation and the data value is imported using that specific representation. If the imported documents with JSON extensions for BSON types do not use convertBsonTypes: true, the documents are imported in the same way as they as represented in the input file, as embedded JSON documents.

- convertBsonOid: Set to true to enable conversion of the MongoDB BSON ObjectId (found in Mongo's extended JSON strict mode) values from 12-byte BSON to a MySQL VARBINARY(32) and used as the **_id** key. . The default is the value of convertBsonTYpes.

- extractOidTime: Set to true to create a new field based on the ObjectID timestamp and this option is only valid if convertBsonOid is enabled. The default is empty. The timestamp

value that is contained in a MongoDB ObjectID in the **_id** field
for a document, and places it into a separate field in the
imported data. The key will be named **extractOidTime** in the
document. The format of the timestamp is that the first 4 bytes
of the ObjectID remains unchanged.

Bson Conversion Options

When convertBsonTypes is enabled, the following options
are available . They are all boolean flags (true or false).
ignoreRegexOptions is enabled by default,rest are disabled by
default.

    - ignoreDate: disables the conversion of BSON Date values.

    - ignoreTimestamp: disables the conversion of BSON
Timestamp values.

    - ignoreRegex: disables the conversion of BSON Regex
values.

    - ignoreBinary: disables the conversion of BSON BinData
values.

    - decimalAsDouble: causes the BSON Decimal values to be
imported as double values.

    - ignoreRegexOptions: causes the regex options to be
ignored when processing a Regex BSON value. This option is only
valid if ignoreRegex is disabled.

If there is not a schema designated then an active schema on the global session, if set, will be used.

Again, the collection and the table options cannot be combined - you can use a collection *OR* you can use a table, not both. If they are not provided, the basename of the file without extension will be used as target *collection* name (default to a collection not table).

BSON Data Type Processing Rules

If only convertBsonOid is enabled there will be no other conversions performed on the rest of the BSON Data Types.

To use extractOidTime, it needs be set to a name which will be used to insert an additional field into the main document. The value of the new field will be the timestamp obtained from the ObjectID value. Note that this will be done only for an ObjectID value associated with the **_id** field of the main document.

NumberLong and NumberInt values will be converted to integer values.

NumberDecimal values will be imported as strings, unless decimalAsDouble is enabled.

Regex values will be converted to strings containing the regular expression. The regular expression options are ignored unless ignoreRegexOptions is disabled. When ignoreRegexOptions is disabled the regular expression will be converted to the form: /<regex>/<options>.

Operating System Shell Usage

Format: mysqlsh user@host:port/mydb --import <path> [target] [tableColumn] [options]

The importJSON utility can be called from the operating system command line interface.

    mysqlsh user@localhost/mydata --import /tmp/salesq1.json

Example 13-15 -- Using the MySQL Shell from the operating system command line to import JSON data.

util.importTable

There is a second utility in MySQShell to import JSON data but it has the ability to work with parallel threads to provide very rapid data import to a MySQL relational table and works very well with large data files. The data file is examined by the utility, divides it into chunks, and uploads those chunks to the MySQL server using parallel connections. This is much faster than the standard single-threaded upload using a LOAD DATA statement.

How Does It Work?

Format: **util.importTable(filename[, options])**

The **importTable** utility was introduced with MySQL Shell 8.0.17 and provides a great deal of control on how the data is uploaded into the database instance. It works on files with DOS CSVs (comma separated values), Unix CSVs, TSVs (tab separated values), and JSON. JSON files must be in the format of one document per line mode. You also can adjust the number of threads, number of bytes sent per each chunk, and the maximum rate of data transfer per thread so you can balance the load on the network and the speed of data transfer.

The parallel table import utility works only on the MySQL Classic Protocol and not the newer X Protocol. The X Protocol connections do not support **LOAD DATA** statements. The parallel table import utility makes use of the **LOAD DATA LOCAL INFILE** statements to upload data chunks from the input file. Make sure that the data file you want to import is in a location that is accessible to the client host as a local disk. Local administrators often secure directories and turn off LOAD DATA as a security precaution so be aware of those potential issues. And the local_infile system variable must be set to **ON** on the target server.

A recommended practice is to return the state back to **OFF** after loading the needed data as a security precaution.

What to specify

Besides the name of your data file you can specify the schema, specify the table name, an array of column names to map to the table in cases where you data file does not have all the columns as the table, designate if you have unique keys (or if you desire duplicates), the termination of individual lines, the terminations of columns, what fields are enclosed by, the number of threads for uploading, the bytes per chunk, the maximum I/O rate, and the dialect of your data file (CSV, TSV, JSON). And you can get a status report on the progress.

Filename

The filename can be more than just the name of a file on the local host. The scheme part of filename can contain information about the transport backend and the supported transport backends include file://, http://, https://, and oci+os://. On Windows systems backslashes can either be escaped in the file path (use \\ with the first \ escaping the second \ character) or forward slashes instead. The data is imported to the MySQL server to which the active MySQL session is connected. The Oracle Cloud Infrastructure (oci) allows you to use this function with servers on the Oracle Cloud with the cloud instances OS (operating system).

Omitting the scheme part of filename causes the file:// transport backend method is selected. The data file to be imported must be in a location that is accessible to the client host as a local disk.

Filename Formats

There are many possible formats for the filename.

`[file://]/path/to/file` is used to read and import data from a system's local file file system. The use of `'file://'` is optional and just the path to the file can be specified and relative pathing is accepted.

`http[s]://host.domain[:port]/path/to/file` can be used to read and import data from file provided in URL.

`oci+os://region/namespace/bucket/object` is for users of the Oracle Cloud Infrastructure (OCI) to read and import data from objects stored in OCI Object Storage. OCI is a separate service from either the MySQL Community Edition or the Enterprise edition. Please refer to the OCI documentation for more usage information in this case.

Options Available

You may specify the name of the *name* of the target *schema* of where data will be written, the table name target *table* to where the data will be uploaded into, or the *columns* where the data is to be stored. The columns option requires a JSON array of column names as its value.

How is the Data Wrapped?

Data columns often constrained and contained by special characters to delineate their start and end. Getting ths encapsulation correct is necessary to ensure the completeness of the data. For Example the last name of O'Hara would be parsed wrong if the system is expecting the ' character in that name as a mark denoting the end of a string. In such cases it is not uncommon for a wide variety of strategies to be used such as "O'Hara", 'O''Hara', 'O'\Hara' among others. And it is not uncommon to find the various fields within a record to be encoded with different measures than the record itself. There is no one 'right way to do this work so flexibility is required to handle different methods.

The *fieldsTerminatedBy* option is a string that defaults to "\t" (also known as TAB character). The *fieldsEnclosedBy* optionis to designate a character (default: '') to designate columns in a record. And the *fieldsEscapedBy* option character (default: '\') is for intra-column data. These options have the same meaning as the corresponding clauses for **LOAD DATA INFILE** command (and this pertains to many of the following options also).

Sometimes the data has multiple encodings and the option (a boolean value, default: false) can be set to true if the input values are not necessarily enclosed within quotation marks specified by the *fieldsEnclosedBy* option. It can be set to false if all fields are quoted by character specified by *fieldsEnclosedBy* option.

Each record needs an end of line character or characters and *linesTerminatedBy* specifies (default: "\n" or NEWLINE character which is the UNIX/Linux default) what they are. For example, to import Windows files will have lines terminated with carriage return and linefeed pairs (\r\n or RETURN followed by a LINEFEED), use --lines-terminated-by="\r\n".

Uploading batches of data that have records that will be redundant in the existing dataset is a headache for many. However potential duplicates can be removed by using *replaceDuplicates*: (default: false). If *replaceDuplicates* is set to TRUE, any input rows that have the same value for a primary key or unique index as an existing row will be replaced. If set to FALSE the duplicate input rows will be skipped.

The *threads* option lets you specify how many threads to use to import the data and the default is eight.

It may be needed to 'cut' the data in the file to be uploaded into small 'chunks' for easier transfer across the network or for consumption by the server. The *bytesPerChunk* option is string (minimum: "131072", default: "50M") specifying the size of these chunks. When used the mysqlsh will send *bytesPerChunk* (plus the bytes to the end of the row) in one single LOAD DATA call. USe the suffixes, k - for Kilobytes (n * 1'000 bytes), M - for Megabytes (n * 1'000'000 bytes), G - for Gigabytes (n * 1'000'000'000 bytes) for clarity and to save typing zeros.

The rate of data being uploaded can teh throttled by the *maxRate* option(default: "0") to limit the data being sent to a throughput upto *maxRate* and measured in bytes per second per thread. Setting *maxRate*="0" means no limit and *maxRate*="4k" limits the rate to four kilobytes per second.

The ability to monitor the performance of this utility can be had by setting showProgress to ture (default: true if you are using a terminal or false otherwise).

Many times data will come with a row of column headers which are probably not needed. Those column headers can be skipped by setting *skipRows* to a positive number. The default is 0 or no rows skipped.

Dialect

The ability to fashion the upload to various common usages is a big benefit. If you consider the type of file being uploaded as a dialect and your data consistently follows the rules of that dialect, then you can benefit greatly by relying on the preconfigured standard for the files data type. The following dialects have been predefined to follow set of options *fieldsTerminatedBy* (FT), *fieldsEnclosedBy* (FE), *fieldsOptionallyEnclosed* (FOE), *fieldsEscapedBy* (FESC) and **linesTerminatedBy** (LT) in following manner:

Default	no quoting, tab-separated, lf line endings. (LT=<LF>, FESC='\', FT=<TAB>, FE=<empty>, FOE=false
CSV	optionally quoted, comma-separated, crlf line endings. (LT=<CR><LF>, FESC='\', FT=",", FE='"', FOE=true
TSV	optionally quoted, tab-separated, crlf line endings. (LT=<CR><LF>, FESC='\', FT=<TAB>, FE='"', FOE=tru

JSON	one JSON document per line. (LT=<LF>, FESC=<empty>, FT=<LF>, FE=<empty>, FOE=false
CSV-UNIX	one JSON document per line. (LT=<LF>, FESC=<empty>, FT=<LF>, FE=<empty>, FOE=false

Using importTable Efficiently

The **importTable()** utility assumes some information that may not be obvious. The data is loaded into the active schema from the global of the current session if a schema is not specified. Be sure to double check your current schema to avoid replacing existing data with new.

Set *fieldsOptionallyEnclosed* to true if the input values are not necessarily enclosed within *fieldsEnclosedBy character*. The LOAD DATA INFILE command cannot interpret the input properly if you specify one separator that is the same as or a prefix of another.

Session connection options that are set in the global session, such as compression, ssl-mode, and the like are used in parallel connections. So do not worry that multiple threads being used to upload data is less secure than a single thread. Each thread uploading a chunk sets the following session variables: **SET unique_checks = 0, SET foreign_key_checks = 0,** and **SET SESSION TRANSACTION ISOLATION LEVEL READ UNCOMMITTED.**

Classic mode needed

The **util.importTable** utility needs to use the older 'classic' MySQL communication protocol as the newer protocol used by the MySQL Shell does not support LOAD DATA functionality. Using the shell with the newer protocol will result in an error.

```
MySQL  localhost:33060+ ssl  demo  JS >
util.importTable("file://D:/dataset/cdcdata.json")
Util.importTable: A classic protocol session is required to
perform this operation. (RuntimeError)
```

Example 13-15 -- You can not use the new shell with the new protocol to use loadTable as the new protocol lacks support for uploading files. A runtime error message will be returned if you attempt to use importTable without the classic protocol. Note the command prompt displays the session is connected to port 33060 which is used by the X Protocol.

Set LOCAL_INFILE

By default the MySQL 8.0 server has the variable LOCAL_INFILE set to 'off' for security reasons. There is some risk in turning this variable to 'ON' and it is recommended by the author that you turn it back to 'OFF' after you finish uploading data. The command to issue in SQL mode is **SET GLOBAL**

LOCAL_INFILE = "ON"; and this needs to be done from a privileged account. Starting with MySQL 8.0.21 the MySQL client library provides the functionality for client applications to restrict local data loading operations to files located in a designated directory and certain MySQL client programs take advantage of this capability.

If the shell session is in JavaScript or Python mode, a command in SQL mode can be made by adding \sql to the SQL statement, such as **\sql SET GLOBAL LOCAL_INFILE = 'ON';**

```
JS > \sql SET GLOBAL LOCAL_INFILE = 'ON';
Fetching table and column names from `demo` for auto-
completion... Press ^C to stop.
Query OK, 0 rows affected (0.0008 sec)
```

Example 13-16 - Setting the LOCAL_INFILE variable from the JavaScript mode by using \sql to issue an SQL mode command.

A table to hold the data needs to be created to house the data and again this SQL command can be entered from JavaScript or Python modes with \sql prepended to the SQL command. In Example 13-17 the table has only one column of type JSON.

```
JS > \sql create table yuser (doc json);
Query OK, 0 rows affected (0.0432 sec)
```

Example 13-17 -- Creating a simple table to house the soon to be uploaded data.

The prerequisites before uploading have now been met and **util.importTable** can be used to upload data.

Using util.importTable

At a minimum the util.importTable function will require the path to the file and the name of the table to store the data. Remember that the table must already exist before the data can be uploaded. Those two arguments are used to invoke the upload such as

util.importTable("/home/dstokes/Downloads/yelp_academic_dataset_user.json",{ "table" : "yuser"}).

```
        JS >
        util.importTable("/home/dstokes/Downloads/yelp_academic_dat
        aset_user.json",{ "table" : "yuser"})
            Importing from file '/home/dstokes/Downloads/yelp_academic_dataset_user.json' to
        table `demo`.`yuser` in MySQL Server at /var%2Frun%2Fmysqld%2Fmysqld.sock using 8 threads
            [Worker003] demo.yuser: Records: 5480   Deleted: 0   Skipped: 0   Warnings: 0
            [Worker001] demo.yuser: Records: 8634   Deleted: 0   Skipped: 0   Warnings: 0
            [Worker000] demo.yuser: Records: 16434   Deleted: 0   Skipped: 0   Warnings: 0
            [Worker004] demo.yuser: Records: 17429   Deleted: 0   Skipped: 0   Warnings: 0
            [Worker005] demo.yuser: Records: 20514   Deleted: 0   Skipped: 0   Warnings: 0
            [Worker002] demo.yuser: Records: 20271   Deleted: 0   Skipped: 0   Warnings: 0
            [Worker007] demo.yuser: Records: 21799   Deleted: 0   Skipped: 0   Warnings: 0
            [Worker006] demo.yuser: Records: 23069   Deleted: 0   Skipped: 0   Warnings: 0XX
        ...
        Worker003] demo.yuser: Records: 18986   Deleted: 0   Skipped: 0   Warnings: 0
            [Worker002] demo.yuser: Records: 21750   Deleted: 0   Skipped: 0   Warnings: 0
            [Worker005] demo.yuser: Records: 41373   Deleted: 0   Skipped: 0   Warnings: 0
            [Worker000] demo.yuser: Records: 74954   Deleted: 0   Skipped: 0   Warnings: 0
        [Worker006] demo.yuser: Records: 66459   Deleted: 0   Skipped: 0   Warnings: 0
        100% (3.27 GB / 3.27 GB), 2.54 MB/s
            File '/home/dstokes/Downloads/yelp_academic_dataset_user.json' (3.27 GB) was imported in
        18 min 36.0670 sec at 2.93 MB/s
        Total rows affected in demo.yuser: Records: 1968703   Deleted: 0   Skipped: 0   Warnings: 0
```

Example 13-18 - Uploading data using util.importTable. In this case a JSON file of data is uploaded into a table named 'yuser'.

From the Command Line Too

You can use the **util.inputTable** utility from within an interactive shell or from a command line. The following is the import of one million rows from a command line.

```
$ mysqlsh mysql://root@localhost --ssl-mode=DISABLED -- util
import-table foo.csv --schema=test --table=foo
Importing from file 'foo.csv' to table `test`.`foo` in MySQL Server at
/var/lib/mysql/mysql.sock using 3 threads
[Worker000] test.foo: Records: 1496823  Deleted: 0  Skipped: 0  Warnings: 0
[Worker001] test.foo: Records: 4204841  Deleted: 0  Skipped: 0  Warnings: 0
[Worker002] test.foo: Records: 4298336  Deleted: 0  Skipped: 0  Warnings: 0
100% (117.80 MB / 117.80 MB), 490.81 KB/s
File 'foo.csv' (117.80 MB) was imported in 2 min 25.9817 sec at 806.94 KB/s
Total rows affected in test.foo: Records: 10000000  Deleted: 0  Skipped: 0
Warnings: 0
```

Example 13-19 -- Using util.importTable from the operating system command line. In this case a CSV file is loaded into a table named 'foo'. And SSl Mode is disabled.

Chapter 11

The MySQL Document Store

Traditionally a developer wanting to use MySQL had to set
up tables, their relations, and maybe their indexes before they
could use the database server. This can require knowledge of
that data that may not be known at the onset of a project. Later
changes to the structure and relations may require extensive and
expensive downtime. With the MySQL Document Store developers no
longer need to worry about performing those steps.

Consider the example below where someone must 1)
authenticate into the MySQL server, 2) create a new schema, 3)
set the current working schema to that new schema, 4) create a
table, and 5) populate that table with data. This is a single
simple table with no tables to relate to or indexes.

```
C:\Program Files\MySQL\MySQL Server 8.0\bin>mysql -u root -
p
Enter password: ******
Welcome to the MySQL monitor.  Commands end with ; or \g.
Your MySQL connection id is 11
Server version: 8.0.21 MySQL Community Server - GPL


Copyright (c) 2000, 2020, Oracle and/or its affiliates. All
rights reserved.


Oracle is a registered trademark of Oracle Corporation
and/or its
```

affiliates. Other names may be trademarks of their
respective
owners.

Type 'help;' or '\h' for help. Type '\c' to clear the
current input statement.

```
mysql> CREATE SCHEMA y1;
Query OK, 1 row affected (0.02 sec)

mysql> USE y1;
Database changed
mysql> CREATE TABLE y (y INT unsigned, doc JSON);
Query OK, 0 rows affected (0.06 sec)
mysql> INSERT INTO y (y,doc) VALUES (1,'{ "test" :
"yes"}');
Query OK, 1 row affected (0.01 sec)

mysql>
```

Chapter 11-1 -- Using the classic protocol to be able to start saving data required several steps.

Comparing the example in 11-1 to 11-2 it is easy to see
that there is no need to define the table before data can be
saved and the JSON data type does not require data
normalization. Since it is not always possible at the beginning
of a project to know what the data will eventually look like at
the end of the project, this can save many headaches. You also
may not have all the data at hand or may need to change the
normalization of the data that is available. Or your data is
purely JSON and you want to keep it that way on the server.

```
C:\Program Files\MySQL\MySQL Server 8.0\bin>mysqlsh
root@localhost
MySQL Shell 8.0.21

Copyright (c) 2016, 2020, Oracle and/or its affiliates. All
rights reserved.
Oracle is a registered trademark of Oracle Corporation
and/or its affiliates.
Other names may be trademarks of their respective owners.

Type '\help' or '\?' for help; '\quit' to exit.
Creating a session to 'root@localhost'
Fetching schema names for autocompletion... Press ^C to
stop.
Your MySQL connection id is 16 (X protocol)
Server version: 8.0.21 MySQL Community Server - GPL
No default schema selected; type \use <schema> to set one.
JS > session.createSchema('y1')
<Schema:y1>
JS > \use y1
Default schema `y1` accessible through db.
JS > db.createCollection('yy')
<Collection:yy>
JS > db.yy.add( { name: "Dave" })
Query OK, 1 item affected (0.1128 sec)
JS >
```

**Example 11-2 -- The MySQL Document Store required fews
steps before data can be saved in the MySQL Server**

The MySQL Document Store is a fast and flexible way to store your data without several of the traditional tasks needed before the database can be used to store data. This provides a quick way to get new projects 'off the ground' and a reliable way to save JSON documents.

JSON Data Type Based

The MySQL JSON data type is extremely flexible. It may be a temptation for some to use the MySQL JSON data type by itself to provide an easy to use, schema less data storage option. Simply having a table with one column and that column being of type JSON would be a very simple solution. Each row could have up to one gigabyte worth of JSON data. This idea is very close to the premise of the MySQL Document Store. And the document store does so much more for you with support for multiple programming languages and the ability to do without Structured Query Language.

The MySQL JSON data type is the foundation of the MySQL Document Store. Relational databases need schemas and columns defined in tables before they can be used. But a document database allows developers to start saving and using data without having predefined data structures. As the data needed evolves for a given application, there is no need to call in a database administrator to redefine tables. It can be as simple as connecting to the MySQL server, selecting schema, selecting a document collection, and storing JSON documents.

JSON provides for embedded arrays and objects and is a solution when the data does not fit into the relational model. There is also no need for an Object Relational Mapper (ORM) layer to map objects in a modern programming language to a column in a table. And this eliminates the need to embed a string with a structured query language query in a program.

Having the Document Store built on the JSON data type allows for the use of the same data as a document database or as a relational database -- at the same time on a single platform. And you can access both collections and tables.

This chapter will be a general introduction as this subject is deserving of its own book (or several). Refer to the MySQL documentation for full details.

By default the MySQL Document Store creates two columns - doc and _id - as per most of the examples in this book. The InnoDB storage engine requires a Primary Key and the _id field provides it. You can of course create your own collections with your own Primary Key.

The X DevAPI

MySQL engineers created a new protocol named the X Protocol to provide functionality the old MySQL protocol lacks. But what are some of the differences? The first is the network connection. Where the traditional protocol listens to TCP/IP port 3306, the new X Protocol listens to port 33060. The X Protocol has a new session model that enables code to scale from a single to multiple servers. And the new protocol requires the use of a new shell -- mysqlsh.

Mysqlsh

The new shell is in anyways similar to the old mysql shell but in others it is a major leap forward. The interface is very similar and familiar but it does so much more. It is built upon the new X DevAPI, has multiple modes, and built in language interpreters for JavaScript & Python, and can also process Structured Query Language (SQL). The new API will allow applications to easily scale from single to multiple server environments, and provide non-blocking asynchronous calls common to many common host languages. The new shell was also designed for server administration for services such as InnoDB CLuster This program is invoked by typing *mysqlsh*.

The X DevAPI session is a higher-level database session idea compared with the traditional lower-level MySQL connections. Sessions can have several MySQL connections and use either the classic MySQL protocol or the new X Protocol. The ClassicSession class provides a low-level MySQL connection to a single MySQL server instance. Applications taking advantage of the new features in the X DevAPI NodeSession class can be run against one or a group of MySQL servers without code changes. NodeSessions provides full support of X DevAPI but limited support of SQL.

So after installation of the new shell, simply type **mysqlsh** to start. By default the session will be in JavaScript mode, designated by the 'JS' in the prompt.

```
JS> db.countryinfo.find('_id = "USA"');
[
    {
        "GNP": 8510700,
        "IndepYear": 1776,
        "Name": "United States",
        "_id": "USA",
        "demographics": {
            "LifeExpectancy": 77.0999984741211,
            "Population": 278357000
        },
        "geography": {
            "Continent": "North America",
            "Region": "North America",
            "SurfaceArea": 9363520
        },
        "government": {
            "GovernmentForm": "Federal Republic",
            "HeadOfState": "George W. Bush"
        }
    }
]
1 document in set (0.00 sec)
JS>
```

Example 11-01 - This example shows use of the MySQL Shell to access the MySQL Document Store to find

a record in the *countryinfo* collection from the *world_x* sample database. In this particular case the document with the *_id* equal to USA is specifically requested. Compare the syntax to the SQL equivalent of *SELECT doc FROM countryindo WHERE doc->"$._id" = 'USA';*

The new shell has three modes -- Python, JavaScript, and SQL -- and acts very similarly to the old shell, especially when in SQL mode. In the above example JavaScript mode is in use and indicated the *JS>* prompt. In the following examples there are cases when the mode is switched to SQL mode.

Connections

The MySQL shell features the ability to connect using the classic MySQL Protocol and the new X DevAPI Protocol. Specifics for the connections use a Uniform Resource Identifier (URI). X protocol connections are TCP only while the classic protocol try to default to Unix sockets.

The URI can be specified on the line starting the shell such as **mysqlsh —uri user:password@host:33060/schema** or you can simply start the shell and then connect with **\connect user@host/schema** (assuming you want to be prompted for the password and the MySQL server is listening to port 33060).

Session Types

There are two types of sessions under the new MySQL Shell. NodeSession are designed for new applications with MySQL servers that support the X DevAPI Protocol (MySQL 5.7.12 or more recent) or the ClassicSession for servers without the X Protocol. All the exciting CRUD and newer features are only available with the NodeSession. At shell invocation, --sqln creates a NodeSession while -sqlc creates a ClassicSession.

After the shell has been started, connections will attempt by default to use the X DevAPI Protocol.

MySQL Shell 8.0.3-labs

Copyright (c) 2016, 2017, Oracle and/or its affiliates. All rights reserved.

Oracle is a registered trademark of Oracle Corporation and/or its affiliates. Other names may be trademarks of their respective owners.

Type '\help' or '\?' for help; '\quit' to exit.

MySQL JS> **\connect dstokes@localhost/world_x**
Creating a session to 'dstokes@localhost/world_x'
Enter password: ******
Your MySQL connection id is 5 (X protocol)
Server version: 5.7.20-log MySQL Community Server (GPL)
Default schema `world_x` accessible through db.
Fetching schema names for auto-completion... Press ^C to stop.
MySQL [localhost+/world_x] JS> **session**
<Session:dstokes@localhost/world_x>
MySQL [localhost+/world_x] JS>

Example 11-2 Connecting after the MySQL shell has been started. Here user dstokes connects to the localhost to access the *world_x* schema.

```
$ mysqlsh root@localhost/world_x
Creating a session to 'root@localhost/world_x'
Enter password: ******
Your MySQL connection id is 8 (X protocol)
Server version: 8.0.3-rc-log MySQL Community Server (GPL)
Default schema `world_x` accessible through db.
Fetching schema names for auto-completion... Press ^C to stop.
MySQL Shell 8.0.3-labs

Copyright (c) 2016, 2017, Oracle and/or its affiliates. All
rights reserved.

Oracle is a registered trademark of Oracle Corporation and/or its
affiliates. Other names may be trademarks of their respective
owners.

Type '\help' or '\?' for help; '\quit' to exit.

 MySQL  localhost:33060+ ssl  world_x  JS >
```

Example 11-3 Connecting with the connection specifics on the command line.

Once you have invoked the shell and logged in, you are ready to get to work.

Collections and Documents

Documents are stored in collections. Collections are containers for documents that hopefully share a purpose. It is easy to create a new collection. Ignoring the details of the new MySQL shells commands for the moment, the following example using the schema *test* is the working document. The session has already been created (the user had logged in to the server). And object named **db** is a global variable assigned to the current active schema. The third bolded command below does the actual creation of a new document collection named 'demo'. Lastly the **getCollections()** function shows us the available collections.

```
JS> \use test
Default schema `test` accessible through db.
JS> db
<Schema:test>
JS> db.createCollection('demo')
<Collection:demo>
JS> db.getCollections();
[
    <Collection:demo>,
    <Collection:foo>
]
MySQL [localhost+/test] JS>
```

Example 11-4 -- This example shows connection to the *test* **schema, referenced as the object** *db*, **and then creating a collection named** *demo*.

163

In the above example, **\use test** tells the server which schema to use. The server uses **db** as a pointer object to point to the chosen schema and issuing **db** by itself confirms it is the selected schema. Next as a collection with the name of *demo*. And finally the **getCollections()** function reports any available collections in the *test* schema. This is using MySQL without the SQL.

Behind the scenes the MySQL server has created the desired collection. To see the work performed is a very simple matter. At the mysqlsh prompt, enter the sql mode by entering **\sql**. Note the prompt will change to *mysql-sh>*. From here on until the shell is exited or the mode is changed again, traditional SQL commands are accepted.

```
JS> \sql
Switching to SQL mode... Commands end with ;
SQL> DESC demo;
+-------+-------------+------+-----+---------+-----------------
+
| Field | Type        | Null | Key | Default | Extra
|
+-------+-------------+------+-----+---------+-----------------
+
| doc   | json        | YES  |     | NULL    |
|
| _id   | varchar(32) | NO   | PRI | NULL    | STORED GENERATED
|
+-------+-------------+------+-----+---------+-----------------
+
2 rows in set (0.01 sec)
```

MySQL [localhost+/test] SQL>

Example 11-5 -- Collection created by db.createCollection('demo') as views from the SQL side of the server. There is a JSON column named *doc* and a VARCHAR column named *_id* that were automatically generated when the collection was created.

A table named demo has been created with two columns. The first column is named *doc* and is in the JSON data type. The second column is a varchar named *_id* that is a stored Generated Column. More details can be seen by using the **SHOW CREATE TABLE demo** command.


```
SQL> SHOW CREATE TABLE demo;
| Table | Create Table
| demo  | CREATE TABLE `demo` (
  `doc` json DEFAULT NULL,
  `_id` varchar(32) GENERATED ALWAYS AS
(json_unquote(json_extract(`doc`,'$._id'
))) STORED NOT NULL,
  PRIMARY KEY (`_id`)
) ENGINE=InnoDB DEFAULT CHARSET=utf8mb4 |
1 row in set (0.00 sec)
SQL>
```


Example 11-6 -- More details of the demo collection providing details on how the *_id* column was created by the use of a generated column.

The *_id* column is generated by extracting and unquoting (with the use of **JSON_EXTRACT** and **JSON_UNQUOTE**) from the JSON document the **_id** key and placing that data in the column. This show be very familiar after the Generated Columns chapter in this publication. Please note that the Document Store will generate a value for the _id value if one is not specified; Specifying your own _id will require a string not a number, i.e. "10" not 10. And having _id designated the Primary Key fulfills the need of the InnoDB storage engine to have a primary key.

CRUD -- Create, Replace, Update, Delete

The MySQL Document store provides functions for CRUD operations -- Create, Replace, Update, and Delete for documents in a collection. They are names add(), modify(), and remove(). These three when combined with find() are the core basic operations most developers need on an ongoing basis to take advantage of the document database.

```
MySQL [localhost+/test] SQL> \js
Switching to JavaScript mode...
MySQL [localhost+/test] JS> db.demo.add({"_id" : "101"})
Query OK, 1 item affected (0.01 sec)
MySQL [localhost+/test] JS> db.demo.find()
[
    {
```

```
    "_id": "101"
    }
]
1 document in set (0.00 sec)
MySQL [localhost+/test] JS>
```

**Example 11-7 -- Adding a document to a collection.
Note that _id is defined as a VARCHAR(32) (see example 11-4
above) and the number 101 has to be a string and that string has
to be in quotes. Note the use of \js to switch to JavaScript
mode from SQL mode.**

The documents in a collection can be acted upon very easily and by a number of functions. These functions have various ways to improve queries.

```
MySQL [localhost+/test] JS>
db.demo.modify("_id='101'").set("shoe",50)
Query OK, 1 item affected (0.01 sec)
MySQL [localhost+/test] JS> db.demo.find("_id='101'")
[
    {
        "_id": "101",
        "shoe": 50
    }
]
1 document in set (0.00 sec)
```

Example 11-8 - Using set to modify a document by adding another key/value pair. In this case the top or root object is extended with the key value pair of *shoe* and *49*. Besides objects, arrays can be added to the document.

```
JS> db.demo.modify("_id='101'").set("feet","[left,right]")
Query OK, 1 item affected (0.01 sec)
MySQL [localhost+/test] JS> db.demo.find("_id='101'")
[
    {
        "_id": "101",
        "feet": "[left,right]",
        "shoe": 50
    }
]
1 document in set (0.00 sec)
MySQL [localhost+/test] JS>
```

Example 11-9 -- Adding an array value to a document

Arrays can also be added to a document with **set**.

```
JS> db.demo.modify("_id='101'").unset("feet")
Query OK, 1 item affected (0.01 sec)
MySQL [localhost+/test] JS> db.demo.find("_id='101'")
[
    {
        "_id": "101",
```

```
        "shoe": 50
    }
]
1 document in set (0.00 sec)
MySQL [localhost+/test] JS>
```

Example 11-10 removing a key/value pair from a document. Note the use of specifying the particular _id to be modified. Without this denoting the exact record to be modified then ALL the documents in the collection would be modified.

The unset function only requires the name of the key of the key/value pair to be deleted. Note the use of the "_id='101'" qualifier in the modify function to specify the exact document to be modified; omission of a way to find the EXACT document to be modified will result in ALL the records in the collection being effected. Note: Be sure to back up your critical data. Retyping documents is laborious, boring, and unproductive.

```
JS> db.demo.modify("_id='101'").set("feet","[left,right]")
Query OK, 1 item affected (0.01 sec)
JS> db.demo.modify("_id='101'").arrayAppend('$.feet',"[toe,arch,heel,ankle]")
Query OK, 1 item affected (0.01 sec)
JS> db.demo.find("_id='101'")
[
    {
        "_id": "101",
        "feet": [
```

```
            "[left,right]",
            "[toe,arch,heel,ankle]"
        ],
        "shoe": 50
    }
]
1 document in set (0.00 sec)
MySQL [localhost+/test] JS>
```

Example 11-11 -- Adding and then appending to an array to a document

Arrays can be appended very easily with arrayAppend and it will append to the end of the array at the key. In Example 11-9, the key *feet* now has two arrays for values associated with it. To append the array [toes, arch, heel, and ankle] to the first array modify the path from "$.feet' to '$.feet[0]' and the result will be [left, right, toes, arch, heel, ankle].

And finally documents can be removed with the **remove()** function. Remember to specify the records or records desired for deletion or ALL the documents in the collection will head for the bit bucket

```
JS> db.demo.remove("_id='101'")
Query OK, 1 item affected (0.01 sec)
JS> db.demo.find()
Empty set (0.00 sec)
JS>
```

Example 11-12 How to remove 1 (one) record and only 1 (one) record that matches the criteria. A crude but effective way of removing duplicate entries.

```
JS> db.demo.add(
        -> {
        -> _id : "101",
        -> first : "Moe",
        -> last : "Howard"
          -> }
          -> )
          ->
Query OK, 1 item affected (0.01 sec)
JS> db.demo.add(
                    -> {
                    -> _id : "201",
                    -> first : "Shemp",
                    -> last : "Howard"
                    -> }
                    -> )
                    ->
Query OK, 1 item affected (0.00 sec)
JS>
```

Example 11-13 Adding records

The add function can accept valid JSON formatted documents on a single or multiple lines. Example 11-11 show entry of two records on multiple lines.

171

Filtering find()

The find() function can be tuned narrow searches or select only certain fields.

```
JS> db.demo.find("last = 'Fine' OR _id = '41'")
[
    {
        "_id": "33",
        "first": "Larry",
        "last": "Fine"
    },
    {
        "_id": "41",
        "first": "Curly",
        "last": "Howard"
    }
]
2 documents in set (0.00 sec)
JS> db.demo.find().fields(["first","last"])
[
    {
        "first": "Moe",
        "last": "Howard"
    },
    {
        "first": "Shemp",
        "last": "Howard"
```

```
    },
    {

        "first": "Larry",

        "last": "Fine"

    },
    {

        "first": "Curly",

        "last": "Howard"

    }
]
4 documents in set (0.00 sec)
JS>
```

Example 11-14 -- find can be modified to narrow down searches and to specify only certain parts of the document are in the returned data.

```
JS> db.demo.find().limit(2)
[
    {

        "_id": "101",

        "first": "Moe",

        "last": "Howard"

    },
    {

        "_id": "201",

        "first": "Shemp",

        "last": "Howard"

    }
```

```
    ]
2 documents in set (0.00 sec)
JS> db.demo.find().limit(2).skip(1)
[
    {
        "_id": "201",
        "first": "Shemp",
        "last": "Howard"
    },
    {
        "_id": "33",
        "first": "Larry",
        "last": "Fine"
    }
]
2 documents in set (0.00 sec)
JS>
```

Example 11-15 -- Limit and Skip functions can also help winnow down returned data

Sorting

The sort function can be added to find to order the returned document. But sort requires that one or or fields in the document be named as a key. With a key named to sort upon the server will send back an *Invalid number of arguments in CollectionFind.sort, expected at least 1 but got 0 (ArgumentError)* error message. If you also use the fields function you need to specify one or more of the returned document keys as the field on which to sort.

```
JS> db.demo.find().fields(["last","first"]).sort("first")
[
    {
        "first": "Curly",
        "last": "Howard"
    },
    {
        "first": "Larry",
        "last": "Fine"
    },
    {
        "first": "Moe",
        "last": "Howard"
    },
    {
        "first": "Shemp",
        "last": "Howard"
    }
]
4 documents in set (0.00 sec)
JS>
```

Example 11-16 -- Sorting can be done but the fields need to be specified to be passed to the sort function. Omitting the field name to be sorted will result in an 'Illegal number of arguments' error message.

```
JS> db.demo.find().sort("_id")
[
    {
        "_id": "101",
        "first": "Moe",
        "last": "Howard"
    },
    {
        "_id": "201",
        "first": "Shemp",
        "last": "Howard"
    },
    {
        "_id": "33",
        "first": "Larry",
        "last": "Fine"
    },
    {
        "_id": "41",
        "first": "Curly",
        "last": "Howard"
    }
]
4 documents in set (0.00 sec)
```

Example 11-17 -- But if fields are not specified then you can just use any key in the document for the sort key

Binding

Binding values to variables is also possible and highly
desirable in scripts when iterating over values. In the
following example a variable is declared by prepending a colon
(:) to the name of the variable. The bind function then
replaces the variable with the value before executing the
command.

```
JS> db.demo.find("last =
:lastname").bind("lastname","Fine")
[
    {
        "_id": "33",
        "first": "Larry",
        "last": "Fine"
    }
]
1 document in set (0.00 sec)
MySQL [localhost+/test] JS>
```

Example 11-18 -- Passing bound parameters

Indexing Collections

Indexes may be added to speed finding specific documents in
a MySQL Document Store just like in the 'regular old MySQL

relational server'. Indexes allow the server to go directly to the record or records desired without having to process every record in the collection. Processing every record is better known as a full table scan and database administrators work hard to eliminate full scans. Sometimes your application does need to read through all the records in a collection in cases like processing all the accounts payables but generally they are to be avoided. Generally one does not read the entire computer manual to answer a single question when the manual has an index that can be used to look up the answer.

Indexes are not a panacea for databases. Indexes are a separate table that needs to be read, maintained as records change or are removed, and managed. It is often tempting to novice database developers to index all columns but the overhead can greatly slow operations.

Indexes are generally unique or not. Unique indexes will have a pointer to one record in the collection. Non unique indexes can have multiple entries. Consider a billing system where each customer will have their own unique identification number but the order collection will hold the identification number of multiple customers.

```
JS> db.demo.createIndex("id_idx").field("_id", "INTEGER",
false).execute()
                            ->
Query OK, 0 items affected (0.10 sec)
JS> \sql
Switching to SQL mode... Commands end with ;
SQL> DESC demo;
```

```
+------------------------------------------------+-------------+------+-----+---
------+------------------+
| Field                                          | Type        | Null | Key | De
fault | Extra            |
+------------------------------------------------+-------------+------+-----+---
------+------------------+
| doc                                            | json        | YES  |     | NU
LL     |                  |
| _id                                            | varchar(32) | NO   | PRI | NU
LL     | STORED GENERATED |
| $ix_i_ED8EA5BF0D44065A674B92033FC24920B41C5F42 | int(11)     | YES  | MUL | NU
LL     | VIRTUAL GENERATED |
+------------------------------------------------+-------------+------+-----+---
------+------------------+
3 rows in set (0.00 sec)
SQL> \js
Switching to JavaScript mode...
JS> db.demo.dropIndex("id_idx").execute()
Query OK, 0 rows affected (0.05 sec)
JS>
```

Example 11-19 -- Creating indexes

The EXPLAIN command can be used in SQL mode but not Python or JavaScript.

```
JS>db.demo.createIndex("last_idx").field("last","TEXT(30)",
false).execute()
Query OK (0.09 sec)
mysql-js>
```

Example 11-20 -- Creating an index but no a unique index

```
JS>db.demo.createIndex("last_idx2",mysqlx.IndexType.UNIQUE)
.field("last" "TEXT(30)",true).execute()
Duplicate entry 'Howard' for key 'last_idx2' (MySQL Error
1062)
JS>
```

Example 11-21 -- Unique indexes can also be created but the field values need to be unique.

```
mysql-js>
db.demo.createIndex("first_idx",mysqlx.IndexType.UNIQUE).fi
eld("first"
,"TEXT(30)",true).execute()
Query OK (0.20 sec)
JS> db.demo.add(
    ... {
    ... _id : "401",
    ... first : "Moe",
    ... last : "Jones"
    ... }
    ... )
    ...
ERROR: 5116: Document contains a field value that is not
unique but required to be
JS>
```

Example 11-22 -- If an UNIQUE index is created any attempt at inserting a duplicate value will produce an error.

Duplication of a key for an unique index will create the error seen in Example 11-20. Sometimes this is caused by trying to add to a document that instead should be modified, other times this can be caused by carelessness. Often you will see MySQL relational tables use an AUTO_INCREMENT definer on a column to have unique values supplied for unique identifiers.

The MySQL Document Store will automatically add a unique _id key if you do not specify a value and use a generated column to build an index. The automatically generated _id's will look like 3019886f8e6fd311640d4851b70943c6 or ac5a657d8e6fd311640d4851b70943c6. You can specify your own _id values (remember they are strings and need quotes around them) and use your own scheme for values.

Dropping a Collection

Data has a lifespan and it is fairly simple to remove or drop a collection. The name of the schema and the name of the collection must be specified.

```
JS> db.getCollections()
[
    <Collection:demo>,
    <Collection:foo>
]
mysql-js> session.dropCollection("test","demo")
Query OK (0.03 sec)
JS> db.getCollections()
[
```

```
        <Collection:foo>
]
JS>
```

Example 11-23 -- Removing the demo collection from the test schema

Once dropped, you can only recover the data from a backup or by re-entering the data, if you have a very good memory.

Chapter 12

Programming with the MySQL Document Store

For decades developers have had to embed Structured Query Language (SQL) as strings in their code or use an Object Relational Mapper (ORM) to be able to use a database. The SQL strings are often esthetically objectionable, sitting in the middle of a beautifully constructed modern program written in a modern programming language. ORMs are often another complexity that can be avoid if developers would learn to properly write SQL.

However there is very little training in SQL, the relational model, or even set theory for most programmers. SQL is a powerful computer language but very few attempt to master it even if they seek highly performing queries.

Developers can use the MySQL Document Store from many programming languages without the need for embedded SQL strings, ORMs, or intensive study in relational databases. It takes away the esthetic complaints and allows those without SQL skills to use the power of MySQL.

The X DevAPI has connectors for most languages. The big change that programmers will quickly notice is that there are no messy strings of SQL queries in the code. Much of the approach is the same as the traditional programming methodology -- authentication to server, designating a schema, issuing a query, and returning the results -- are the same but the code looks much cleaner.

As of the writing of this book, MySQL provides connectors for Java (Connector/J), C++, Node.js, .Net, and Python. A PECL extension for PHP in available. The MySQL connectors are available from the MySQL website and the PHP PECL extension is available from the PECL.PHP.Net website. More connectors may be available at a later date.

Programming Examples

Python Example

The following example is in Python but is a typical example of the coding style when using the X DevAPI.

```python
import mysqlx

# Connect to server on localhost
session = mysqlx.get_session({
    'host': 'localhost',
    'port': 33060,
    'user': 'dave',
    'password': 'S3cR3T!',
    'ssl-mode' : mysqlx.SSLMode.DISABLED #Remove this
line if SSL enabled
})

schema = session.get_schema('world_x')

# Use the collection 'countryinfo'
collection = schema.get_collection('countryinfo')

# Specify which document to find with
Collection.find()
result = collection.find('_id like
:param').bind('param', 'USA').execute()

# Print document
docs = result.fetch_all()
print('id: {0}'.format(docs[0]['Name']))
```

Example 12-1 -- An example of using the MySQL Document Store with the MySQL X DevAPI Python Connector

Node.JS Example

Similar code in Node.JS will also seem very familiar after Chapter 11. The language differences between Node.JS and Python are still evident but the X DevAPI code -- **getCollection(), find()** -- remains the same.

```
// Simple example to grab one record and print it
const mysqlx = require('@mysql/xdevapi');
const options = {
  host: 'localhost',
  port: 33060,
  dbUser: 'dave',
  dbPassword: 'S3cR3t!!'
};

mysqlx
  .getSession(options)
  .then (session => {
  var schema = session.getSchema('world_x');

//equivalent of SELECT doc FROM countryinfo where _id
= 'USA'
  var coll = schema.getCollection('countryinfo');
  var query = "$._id == 'USA'";
```

```
          // Print doc
      return Promise.all([
        coll.find(query).execute(function (doc) {
        console.log(doc);
       }),
       session.close()
      ]);
     })
    .catch(err => {
        console.log(err.message);
        console.log(err.stack);
    });
```

Example 12-2 -- The equivalent code in Node.JS retains the familiar X DevAPI function calls and is very similar to the code written in Python in Example 12-1.

PHP Example

PHP is a very popular web programming language and once again the code looks similar to previous examples.

```
#!/usr/bin/php
<?PHP
// Connection parameters
  $user = 'dave';
  $passwd = 'S3cR3t!';
  $host = 'localhost';
```

```php
  $port = '33060';
  $connection_uri =
'mysqlx://'.$user.':'.$passwd.'@'.$host.':'.$port;
  echo $connection_uri . "\n";


// Connect as a Node Session
  $nodeSession =
mysql_xdevapi\getNodeSession($connection_uri);
// "USE world_x"
  $schema = $nodeSession->getSchema("world_x");
// Specify collection to use
  $collection = $schema->getCollection("countryinfo");


// Query the Document Store
  $result = $collection->find('_id = "USA"')->fields(['Name
as Country','geography as Geo','geography.Region'])-
>execute();


// Fetch/Display data
  $data = $result->fetchAll();
  var_dump($data);
?>
```

Example 12-3 -- The X DevAPI calls retain familiar format despite the code now being in PHP.

A Side By Side Comparison of Traditional SQL and Document Server

The MySQL Document Store also allows developers to choose between the traditional SQL approach and the Document Store. Example 12-4 has the same code in PHP side by side.

Traditional	Document Store

<pre><?PHP
// Connection parameters
$host='127.0.0.1';
$user='dave';
$pass='S3cR3t!';
$db = 'world_x';
 	
// connect to database server
$mysqli =
mysqli_connect('localhost','root','hidave');
 	
// Choose schema
$mysqli->select_db('world_x');
 	
// send SQL query</pre>
	<pre><?PHP
	// Connection parameters
	  $user = 'dave';
	  $passwd = 'S3cR3t!';
	  $host = 'localhost';
	  $port = '33060';
	
	  $connection_uri =
	'mysqlx://'.$user.':'.$passwd
	.'@'.$host.':'.$port;
	
	// Connect as a Node Session
	  $nodeSession =
	mysql_xdevapi\getNodeSession(
	$connection_uri);
	
	// Choose schema
	  $schema = $nodeSession-
	>getSchema("world_x");
	// Specify collection to use
	  $collection = $schema-
	>getCollection("countryinfo")
	;</pre>

```
if ($result = $mysqli-                  $result = $collection-
>query("SELECT doc FROM               >find('_id = "USA"')-
countryinfo WHERE _id='USA'")) {      >execute();
    $row =                               $data = $result-
mysqli_fetch_row($result);            >fetchAll();
    var_dump($row);                      var_dump($data);
}                                     ?>
?>
```

Example 12-4 -- The same program written in PHP with
the traditional SQL query on the left and the MySQL Document
Store on the right.

Developers can use either the traditional SQL or the MySQL
Document Store, or both. It would not be a good programming
practice to

The MySQL Shell and JavaScript

The new MySQL Shell (mysqlsh) also has modes for JavaScript and Python. It is very easy to start up the shell and simply enter code.

MySQL Shell 1.0.11

Type '\help' or '\?' for help; '\quit' to exit.

Currently in JavaScript mode. Use \sql to switch to SQL mode and execute queries
.
```
mysql-js> var mysqlx = require('mysqlx');
mysql-js> var mySession = mysqlx.getNodeSession( {
      ... host: 'localhost', port: 33060, dbUser : 'root',
dbPassword : 'hidave'
});
      ...
mysql-js> var db = mySession.getSchema('test');
mysql-js> var foo = db.createCollection('foobarx');
mysql-js> foo.add({name : "Dave", location :
"Texas"}).execute();
Query OK, 1 item affected (0.01 sec)
mysql-js>
```

```
mysql-js> var document = foo.find().execute();
mysql-js> print(document.fetchOne());
{
    "_id": "27190ac58976d31184064851b70943c6",
    "location": "Texas",
    "name": "Dave"
}
mysql-js>
```

Example 12-5 -- It is also very simple to use the built in JavaScript or Python interpreters with the MySQL shell to quickly store JSON documents or programmatically access data.

Relational Tables

The MySQL Document Store can also be used to access relational tables or treat collections as tables.

Chapter 13

Multi-Value Indexes

Before MySQL 8.0.17 you could store data in JSON arrays but trying to search on that data in those embedded arrays was tricky and usually required a full table scan. And full table scans are s-l-o-w.

Multi-valued indexes are intended for indexing JSON arrays. Creating a multi-valued index or MVI is done with a **CREATE TABLE, ALTER TABLE,** or **CREATE INDEX** statement. The **CAST(... AS ... ARRAY)** function is used in the index definition to cast as same-typed scalar values in a JSON array to an SQL data type array.Please note the same-type values is a requirement and you can not mix other types of values into this index. Next the system creates a virtual column for the various values. And finally, a functional index, also known as a virtual index, is created on this new virtual column.

The following example takes the arrays found at the key 'nbr' from the JSON document in the column named 'j' and places it into an index named 'nbrs' . Note the casting of the **$.nbr** key/values as an unsigned array.

```
MySQL  localhost:33060+ ssl  test  SQL > CREATE TABLE s (id INT UNSIGNED AUTO_INCREMENT PRIMARY KEY,
                                    ->        name CHAR(20) NOT NULL,
                                    ->        j JSON,
                                    ->        INDEX nbrs( (CAST(j->'$.nbr' AS UNSIGNED ARRAY)))
                                    ->        );
Query OK, 0 rows affected (0.1600 sec)
MySQL  localhost:33060+ ssl  test  SQL >
```

mysql> CREATE TABLE s (id INT UNSIGNED AUTO_INCREMENT PRIMARY
KEY,

    -> name CHAR(20) NOT NULL,

    -> j JSON,

    -> **INDEX nbrs((CAST(j->'$.nbr' AS UNSIGNED ARRAY)))**

    ->);

Query OK, 0 rows affected (0.11 sec)

Example 14 - 1 - Creating a table with a multi-value index with data from a JSON document.

Then add in some data. The goal is to have a set of multiple values available under the 'nbr' key where each number in the array represents some enumerated attribute.

Mysql> **SELECT * FROM s;**

```
+----+-------+--------------------+
| id | name  | j                  |
+----+-------+--------------------+
|  1 | Moe   | {"nbr": [1, 7, 45]} |
|  2 | Larry | {"nbr": [2, 7, 55]} |
|  3 | Curly | {"nbr": [5, 8, 45]} |
|  4 | Shemp | {"nbr": [3, 6, 51]} |
+----+-------+--------------------+
```
4 rows in set (0.00 sec)

Example 14 -2 -- Example data for Multi valued indexes.

The **MEMBER OF()** that can take advantage of MVIs. Searching for values is shown below.

```
MySQL  localhost:33060+ ssl  test  SQL > SELECT * FROM s WHERE 7 MEMBER OF (j->"$.nbr");
+----+-------+------------------+
| id | name  | j                |
+----+-------+------------------+
|  1 | Moe   | {"nbr": [1, 7, 45]} |
|  2 | Larry | {"nbr": [2, 7, 55]} |
+----+-------+------------------+
2 rows in set (0.0007 sec)
MySQL  localhost:33060+ ssl  test  SQL >
```

mysql> **SELECT * FROM s WHERE 7 MEMBER OF (j->"$.nbr");**

```
+----+-------+--------------------+
| id | name  | j                  |
+----+-------+--------------------+
|  1 | Moe   | {"nbr": [1, 7, 45]} |
|  2 | Larry | {"nbr": [2, 7, 55]} |
+----+-------+--------------------+
```

2 rows in set (0.00 sec)

Example 14 - 3 -- Example data for Multi valued indexes

In this example data there are two records with the number 7 in the array. Think about how many times you have multiple uses of things like postal codes, phone numbers, credit cards , or email addresses tied to a master record. Rather than having multiple records in child tables, you can keep all that within one JSON document and not have to make multiple dives into the data to retrieve that information. Imagine you have a 'build sheet' of a complex product, say a car, and you wanted to be able to quickly find the ones with certain attributes (GPS, tinted windows, and red leather seats). A MVI gives you a way to quickly and efficiently search for these attributes.

And for those curious about the query plan:

```
mysql> EXPLAIN SELECT * FROM s WHERE 7 MEMBER OF (j->"$.nbr")\G
*************************** 1. row ***************************
           id: 1
  select_type: SIMPLE
        table: s
   partitions: NULL
         type: ref
possible_keys: nbrs
          key: nbrs
      key_len: 9
          ref: const
         rows: 1
     filtered: 100.00
        Extra: Using where
1 row in set, 1 warning (0.00 sec)
```

Example 14 - 4 -- The query plan clear shows 'nbrs' is used as the key (index) for the query.

And yes the optimizer handles the Multi value index easily.

MVIs are great for searching arrays but there are some implementation notes below that you will want to familiarize yourself with to make sure you know all the fine points of using MVIs.

- Only one MVI can be used in a composite index.

- You can use **MEMBER OF, JSON_CONTAINS(),** or **JSON_OVERLAPS()** in the WHERE clause to take advantage of MVIs. But once again you can use those three functions on non MVI JSON Data too.

- The Data Manipulation Language or DML for MVIs work like the DMLs for other types of Indexes but you may have more than one insert/updates for a single clustered index record. Each row inserted, updated, or deleted in the data table can produce many more rows to be inserted into the index and that overhead can eat into the performance of the query. Monitor this workload to see if it has too much of an impact.

- Empty arrays are not added to the index so do not try to search for empty values via the index.

- MVIs do not support ordering of values so do not use them for primary keys! And no ascending (ASC) or descending (DSC) attributes either!!

- You are limited to 644,335 keys and 10,000 bytes by InnoDB for a single record. The limit is a single InnoDB undo log page size so you should get up to 1250 integer values in that log page.

- MVIs can not be used in a foreign key specification.

And check the cardinality of your data. Having a very narrow range of numbers indexed will not really gain extra performance. An index will not speed up your queries if there are only a few unique values in that index.

A Bigger Example

Lets create a table with one million rows with randomly created data inside a JSON array. Let us use a very simple table with a primary key and a JSON column that will supply the JSON array for the secondary index.

```
mysql>desc a1;
+-------+-------------------+------+-----+---------+----------------+
| Field | Type              | Null | Key | Default | Extra          |
+-------+-------------------+------+-----+---------+----------------+
| id    | int(10) unsigned  | NO   | PRI | NULL    | auto_increment |
| data  | json              | YES  |     | NULL    |                |
+-------+-------------------+------+-----+---------+----------------+
2 rows in set (0.00 sec)
```

Example 14 - 5 -- An example table for MVI evaluation

The following PHP script can be used to generate data on STDOUT to a temporary file. Bash or another programming language can be used as well. The script is run and the output redirected to a flat file. And that temporary file was fed in using the MySQL source command. It is the author's personal preference to load data this way as it does allow you to truncate or drop table definitions and re-use the same data.

```php
<?php

for ($x=1; $x < 1000000; $x++) {
    $i = rand(1,10000000);
$j = rand(1,10000000);
$k = rand(1,10000000);
echo "INSERT into a1 (id,data) VALUES (
    NULL,'{\"nbr\":[$i,$j,$k]}');\n";
```

```
}
?>
```

Example 14 - 6 -- Simple script written in PHP to generate test data.

An example line from the file looks like this:

```
INSERT into a1 (id,data) VALUES
(NULL,'{"nbr":[8526189,5951170,68]}');
```

Example 14 - 7 -- An example line generated from the script in Example 14 - 6.

The entries in the array should have a pretty large cardinality with ranges between 1 and 10,000,000, especially considering there are only 1,000,000 rows. It is very easy to alter the script for more or less rows of data.

Array subscripts in JSON start with a 0 (zero). And remember that the way to get to the third item in the array would be **SELECT data->>"$.nbr[2]"**. Without a MVI, checking the data from $.nbr[0] to $.nbr[N] we would have to explicitly check each one. Not pretty and expensive to perform.
Testing MVI

It is good practice to see what the optimizer wants to do to develop a query plan and the use of EXAMINE prepended to a query is the traditional tool for this work. The example used here is a simple search for a $.nbr[0] = 99999 row in the table

is used here as an example. One record with all three elements
in the array as five nines to make for a simple example.

The example query is listed below as Example 14 - 10.


```
*************************** 1. row ***************************
          id: 1
 select_type: SIMPLE
       table: a1
  partitions: NULL
        type: ALL
possible_keys: NULL
         key: NULL
     key_len: NULL
         ref: NULL
        rows: 9718585
    filtered: 100
       Extra: Using where
1 row in set, 1 warning (0.0004 sec)
Note (code 1003): /* select#1 */ select `test`.`a1`.`id` AS
`id`,json_unquote(json_extract(`test`.`a1`.`data`,'$.nbr')) AS
`data->>"$.nbr"` from `test`.`a1` where
(json_unquote(json_extract(`test`.`a1`.`data`,'$.nbr[0]')) =
99999)
```
Example 14-8 -- The query plan without an MVI

And there are no indexes available to be used and it is a
full table scan, as indicated in the type: ALL above. The query
runs in about 0.61 seconds on a test laptop and this could be
considered the worst case scenario.

In the previous example we created the index with the table but this time it is created after the table. And I could have used ALTER TABLE too.

CREATE INDEX data__nbr_idx ON a1((CAST(data->'\$.nbr' AS UNSIGNED ARRAY)));

Example 14-9 -- Using Alter Table to create the Multi value index

So first trial query:

SELECT id, data->>"\$.nbr"
FROM a
WHERE data->>"\$.nbr[2]" = 99999

EXAMPLE 14-10 -- The sample query

We have to pick a specific entry in the array as we can not search each item of the array (at least until we can use MVIs). Since that data was 'seeded' with one record that we know will match, we know that the server will return at least one matching row. The query runs in about 0.62 seconds, or a fraction slower but close enough to say they are the same time. And **EXPLAIN** shows this is a full table scan and it does not take advantage of that index just created. So how do we access this new index and take advantage of the MVIs?

New Functions To The Rescue

There are new functions that can take advantage of MVIs when used to the right of the WHERE clause in a query with InnoDB tables. One of those functions is **MEMBER OF()**. The test query is modified slightly to accommodate the new function.

SELECT _id, data->>"$.nbr"
FROM a1
WHERE 99999 MEMBER OF (data->"$.nbr");

   Example 14-11 -- Using MEMBER OF to take advantage of the MVI

This query runs in 0.001 seconds which is much faster than the previous time of 0.61! And we are searching all the data in the array, not just one slot in the array. So if we do not know if the data we want is in $.nbr[0] or $.nbr[N], we can search all of the array entries easily. So we are actually looking at more data and at a much faster rate.

We can also use **JSON_CONTAINS()** and **JSON_OVERLAPS()** see Three New JSON Functions in MySQL 8.0.17 fro details. These three functions are designed to take full advantage of Multi-Value indexes.

SELECT id, data->>"$.nbr"
FROM a1
WHERE JSON_CONTAINS(data->'$.nbr',
   cast('[99999,99999]' as JSON));

```
+---------+----------------------+
| id      | data->>"$.nbr"       |
+---------+----------------------+
| 1000000 | [99999, 99999, 99999] |
```

```
+---------+----------------------+
```
1 row in set (0.0013 sec)

Example 14 - 12 -- Using JSON_CONTAINS() to find a record in the test data set.


```
SELECT id, data->>"$.nbr"  FROM a1  WHERE
JSON_OVERLAPS(data->'$.nbr',cast('[99999,99999]' as JSON)
);
+---------+----------------------+
| id      | data->>"$.nbr"       |
+---------+----------------------+
| 1000000 | [99999, 99999, 99999] |
+---------+----------------------+
1 row in set (0.0012 sec)
```

Example 14 - 13 -- Using JSON_OVERLAP() to fins a record in the test data set.

Chapter 15

JSON Document Validation

JSON has been adopted by most of the major database software vendors much to the chagrin of traditional Database Administrators and developers. Relational Databases have been built on the framework of a pretty rigid framework where the data has been normalized and there is no way to put, for example, a string into an integer field. The NoSQL JSON Document way has no such formal schema.

Many in the relational world have complained that the NoSQL approach does not allow you to have rigor applied to your data. That is to make sure an integer value is really an integer and within specified ranges or string of the proper length. And there was no way to make sure that email addresses are not listed under a combination of E-mail, e-mail, eMail, and eMAIL. JSON is great for many things but traditional, normalized data was better for making certain that your data matched what was specified.

It is much less expensive in terms of time and money to keep bad data out than having to correct it later. The ability to enforce order on incoming data is a great advantage for many DBAs.

MySQL 8.0.17 added the ability to validate JSON documents against a schema following the guidelines of the JSON-Schema.org's fourth draft standard. This provides a way to have required fields, data range checks, and data type checks applied to the data before it is conferred to the database.

Valid JSON and Really Valid JSON

As mentioned in the second chapter of this book, the MySQL server will reject an invalid JSON document when using the JSON data type. But there is a difference between syntactically valid and validation against a schema. With schema validation you can define how the data should be formatted and specify which fields are required. This will help with automated testing using constraint checks and help ensure the quality of your data.

Overly Simple Example

Example 15-1 is a simple document schema that looks at a key named 'myage' and sets up rules that the minimum value is 28 and the maximum value is 99. This document is used as an exemplar or model to benchmark other records against for validity.

```
set @s='{"type": "object",
    "properties": {
    "myage": {
        "type" : "number",
        "minimum": 28,
        "maximum": 99
```

```
      }
    }
}';
```

Example 15-1 - This document is used to make sure that all documents checked against it have an object named 'myage' and that 'myage' is a numeric value between 28 and 99.

And the test document where we use a value for 'myage' that is between the minimum and the maximum.

```
set @d='{  "myage": 33}';
```

Example 15-2 -- The test data

The function **JSON_SCHEMA_VALID()** is used to test if the test document passes the validation test, with 1 or true as a pass and 0 or false as a fail.

```
select JSON_SCHEMA_VALID(@s,@d);
+--------------------------+
| JSON_SCHEMA_VALID(@s,@d) |
+--------------------------+
|                        1 |
+--------------------------+
1 row in set (0.00 sec)
```

Example 15-3 -- The test data in @d has been validated against the exemplar document @s and JSON_SCHEMA_VALID() returns a 1 or true as its return code.

It is a wise practice to test with data that will fail the test to ensure that the test is valid. The test can be tried again with a non-numeric value.

```
set @d='{  "myage": "foo"}';
```

Example 15-4 -- Test document with data that will fail validation.

```
mysql> select JSON_SCHEMA_VALID(@s,@d);
+--------------------------+
| JSON_SCHEMA_VALID(@s,@d) |
+--------------------------+
|                        0 |
+--------------------------+
```

Example 15-5 -- The invalid document when tested returns a 0 or false, as expected.

Testing should be complete and include a value below the minimum.

```
mysql> set @d='{  "myage": 16}';
Query OK, 0 rows affected (0.00 sec)

mysql> select JSON_SCHEMA_VALID(@s,@d);
+--------------------------+
| JSON_SCHEMA_VALID(@s,@d) |
+--------------------------+
|                        0 |
+--------------------------+
```

```
1 row in set (0.00 sec)
```

Example 15-6 -- Testing below the minimum acceptable numeric value also fails

Validity Report

We can use **JSON_SCHEMA_VALIDATION_REPORT()** to get more information on why a document is failing with **JSON_SCHEMA_VALID()**. Receiving a 0 or false from **JSON_SCHEMA_VALID()** does not confer why it failed. To determine that information another function is needed.

```
mysql> select JSON_SCHEMA_VALIDATION_REPORT(@s,@d)\G
*************************** 1. row
***************************
JSON_SCHEMA_VALIDATION_REPORT(@s,@d): {"valid": false,
"reason": "The JSON document location '#/myage' failed
requirement 'minimum' at JSON Schema location
'#/properties/myage'", "schema-location":
"#/properties/myage", "document-location": "#/myage",
"schema-failed-keyword": "minimum"}
1 row in set (0.00 sec)
```

Example 15-7 -- JSON_SCHEMA_VALIDATION_REPORT() not only provides information that the document validation failed by the reasons why it failed.

Please note that the response is in JSON format which can be parsed by the receiving program. And you can neaten the output up with **JSON_PRETTY()** wrapped around the above query.

```
select JSON_PRETTY(JSON_SCHEMA_VALIDATION_REPORT(@s,@d))\G
*************************** 1. row ***************************
JSON_PRETTY(JSON_SCHEMA_VALIDATION_REPORT(@s,@d)): {
  "valid": false,
  "reason": "The JSON document location '#/myage' failed
requirement 'minimum' at JSON Schema location
'#/properties/myage'",
  "schema-location": "#/properties/myage",
  "document-location": "#/myage",
  "schema-failed-keyword": "minimum"
}
```

Example 15-8 -- Pretty printed report for human eyes.

Required Keys

If you want to make sure certain keys are included in a document, you can use the *required* option in your schema definition. So if you are working with GIS information, you can specify requiring longitude and latitude.

```
"required": ["latitude", "longitude"]
```

**Example 15-9 -- Adding 'required' will cause the
server to make sure that the key or keys specified are included
in the document to be validated.**

So we can not have required fields and specify their value
ranges. And it can be ensured BEFORE committing the JSON
document to the MySQL server that the data conforms to our
schema.

Automatic Document Validation with Constraint Checks

SO the next logical step is to use the **CONSTRAINT CHECK**
option on table creation (or alter table) to assure that the
server not only gets a valid JSON document but a verified JSON
document.

Constraint Checks have been part of the MySQL syntax for a
very long time but it has only been relatively recently that
they have actually been enabled to work. The concept behind
them is that the column's data is tested to see if it passes a
test and only when passed will the server allow the data into
the database instance.

```
SQL > CREATE TABLE mycheck (x INT
              CONSTRAINT x_gt_0 CHECK (x>0)
);
Query OK, 0 rows affected (0.0466 sec)
```

```
SQL > INSERT INTO mycheck (x) VALUES (1);
Query OK, 1 row affected (0.0161 sec)
SQL > INSERT INTO mycheck (x) VALUES (-1);
ERROR: 3819: Check constraint 'x_gt_0' is violated.
```

Example 15-10 -- Using a CONSTRAINT CHECK to ensure that a column matches a predefined criteria before the server will accept a row of data.

CONSTRAINED JSON

JSON_SCHEMA_VALID() can easily be added as a constraint check in a table definition. Since **JSON_SCHEMA_VALID()** returns a 1 or true if the document passes the validation check then it is easy to add a constraint check.

```
CREATE TABLE `testx` (
 `col` JSON,
CONSTRAINT `myage_inRange`
CHECK (JSON_SCHEMA_VALID('{"type": "object",
     "properties": {
      "myage": {
     "type" : "number",
     "minimum": 28,
      "maximum": 99
      }
},"required": ["myage"]
 }', `col`) = 1)
);
```

Example 15-11 -- A constraint named 'myage_inRange' is created to make sure that object named 'myage' is a numeric value between the values of 28 and 99. And the document is required to have a key/value pair named 'myage'. If any of those are missing the document will not be added.

And the proof that it works.

```
mysql> insert into testx values('{"myage":27}');
    ERROR 3819 (HY000): Check constraint 'myage_inRange'
is violated.
mysql> insert into testx values('{"myage":97}');
Query OK, 1 row affected (0.02 sec)
```

Example 15-12 -- An age entered that is too low will fail the constraint check while data that is acceptable is added to the instance.

Boolean & String Validation

Boolean data and strings can also be validated. The first example showed how to validate numeric data.

Boolean values are true or false. They have many uses despite being so logically simple. In the following example the JSON data is checked for the presence of a key named *nda_filed* and if its boolean value is either true or false by specifying the type as bolean. Values other than true or false are rejected.

```
CREATE TABLE `testx` (
    `col` json DEFAULT NULL,
    CONSTRAINT `myage_inRange`
    CHECK ((json_schema_valid(
        '{"type": "object",
            "properties": {"nda_filed":
                { "type" :"boolean"}
    },
        "required":  ["nda_filed"]
}', `col`) = 1))
    );
```

```
mysql> INSERT INTO testx (col)
    VALUES ('{ "id" : 1, "nda_filed" : true }');
Query OK, 1 row affected (0.02 sec)
mysql> INSERT INTO testx (col)
    VALUES ('{ "id" : 2, "nda_filed" : "not yet" }');
ERROR 3819 (HY000): Check constraint 'myage_inRange' is
violated.
mysql> INSERT INTO testx (col) VALUES ('{ "id" : 6 }');
ERROR 3819 (HY000): Check constraint 'myage_inRange' is
violated.
mysql>
```

Example 15-13 -- Checking JSON data for boolean values

Strings can contain many different values including
letters, numbers, and much more. To ensure a JSON object has
string data set the type value to string as in Example 15-14.

```
CREATE TABLE `test17` (
    `col` JSON,
```

```
      CONSTRAINT `email_not_string`
      CHECK (JSON_SCHEMA_VALID('{"type": "object",
         "properties": {
            "email": {
               "type" : "string"
            }
         },"required": ["email"]
      }', `col`) = 1)
   );


mysql> INSERT INTO test17 (col) VALUE ('{ "email" : 123}');
ERROR 3819 (HY000): Check constraint 'email_not_string' is
violated.
mysql> INSERT INTO test17 (col)
      VALUE ('{ "email" :"me@me.net"}');
Query OK, 1 row affected (0.01 sec)
mysql>
```

Example 15-14 -- Checking JSON object to see if it is a string with JSON_VALID_SCHEMA()

JSON schema validation removes some of the big criticisms on using JSON in a relational database. The ability to rigorously test data and keep bad data out of the database is a paramount goal for database administrators and developers. **JSON_SCHEMA_VALID()** provides a way to check for the existence of a key, test the data type of the specified value, and specify that the value is required. And when paired with constraint checks it becomes a valuable tool for proving the quality of the data being stored. While not as easy to do as with normalized relational data, this is a huge win for those using JSON.

Epilogue

This book started with 'once upon a time' and I would like to have it end with 'they lived happily ever after'. The engineers at MySQL and Contributors from the MySQL Community have put a lot of effort into the JSON data type and the supporting functions. New uses such as the MySQL Document Store will hopefully bring new changes. JSON and MySQL combine to make a lot of things very convenient for developers and the future should only improve. Thus allowing all involved to live happily ever after.

Appendix A

The MySQL X DevAPI relies on the Google Protocol Buffers which
are a language and platform neutral method for defining the
storage of data. Ways to pass data are defined and the Protocol
Buffer Compiler builds classes for use within programming
languages. Additions to the ways to pass data can be made and
backward compatibility is not lost.

When compiling the X DevAPI code from source code you will need
to download and build the Google Protocol Buffer Software. You
may also need to build this code when using re-packaged
connectors. Pre-built Google Protocol Buffer Software may exists
for the operating system of your choice but just in case please
refer to the following website.

https://developers.google.com/protocol-buffers/

Appendix B - The *world_x* database , MySQL Labs software, JSON
Data Sets and more

The *world_x* database is an evolution of the *world* database
used by MySQL for decades in documentation, classes, and blogs
for many years. https://dev.mysql.com/doc/index-other.html

MySQL from time releases software that is an early glimpse
into possible future software releases. This software is for
testing only and highly NOT recommended for production. Treat
it as a proof of concept and provide any feedback you can; the
experimental code may not make it into production.
https://labs.mysql.com/

There are many great example data sets in JSON to
experiment with to help develop proficiency. The Zip code data
and other great sets are available at:
http://jsonstudio.com/resources/

The jq command line JSON parser can be found at
https://stedolan.github.io/jq/

The example MongoDB dataset is found at
https://raw.githubusercontent.com/mongo/docs-assets/primer-
dataset/primer-dataset.json

Thanks To:

My wife Carrie Stokes. In 2017 I rode over 85,000 miles on American Airlines alone and went to too many conferences. And then when I get home I start spending more time closed away in my office to finish this book! She put up with a lot for my career and for this book and needs a big thanks.

Then in 2020 I told her I wanted to update the material for a second edition. Now the book is done for a second time and I get the opportunity to spend more time with her.

My coworkers. I joined MySQL as a PHP Programmer in the Certification Division in 2007 after using the database for many years. Every MySQL-er has impressed me greatly and I regularly feel like the dim bulb in a sea of shining neon lasers when we get together. To say MySQL has grown and thrived through the efforts of many persons is an understatement and I am frankly humbled (and surprised) to be around you all.

The MySQL Community. I am routinely set to slack jaw yokel mode when talking to members of the MySQL Community when they tell me what they are doing with this incredible database. You folks routinely come up with new ways and combinations of using MySQL that impress me.

Chapter 1

JSON Document Validation

Epilogue

Made in the USA
Columbia, SC
18 February 2025

54063752R00122